An American Adviser
in Late Yi Korea

An American Adviser
in Late Yi Korea:
The Letters of
Owen Nickerson Denny

EDITED, WITH AN INTRODUCTION, BY
Robert R. Swartout, Jr.

THE UNIVERSITY OF ALABAMA PRESS

*The two Chinese characters on the title page
represent Denny's name and are taken
directly from his official commission as
adviser to King Kojong.*

*The device used on the part titles is a
royal seal of the Yi Dynasty.*

Library of Congress Cataloging in Publication Data

Denny, O. N.
    An American adviser in late Yi Korea.

    Includes the text of China and Korea.
    Bibliography: p.
    Includes index.
    1. Korea—History—1864–1910. 2. Korea—Relations
—China. 3. China—Relations—Korea. 4. Denny, O. N.
5. Government consultants—Korea—Correspondence.
6. Americans—Korea—Correspondence. 7. Korea—
Officials and employees, Alien—Correspondence.
I. Swartout, Robert R., 1946–   . II. Denny, O. N.
China and Korea. 1984. III. Title.
DS915.15.D46 1984   951.9'02   83-5042
ISBN 0-8173-0189-5

To

Mr. William C. Ralston

and

Mrs. Stephanie Scott Williams

Contents

Illustrations follow page 51.

Editor's Preface

From 1886 to 1890 Owen Nickerson Denny, an American from the state of Oregon, served as adviser to Korea's King Kojong. During this period Denny held two official positions simultaneously in the Korean government: Director of Foreign Affairs, and Vice-President of the Home Office. The latter position was especially important, as it provided him with access to the King. Denny proved to be one of the most important as well as one of the most controversial Western advisers to serve the Korean government in the last decades of the Yi dynasty.

The letters of Owen N. Denny in this volume have been selected for two general reasons. First, they help to illustrate the scope, along with some of the limitations, of Denny's activities in Korea. Second, the letters broaden our understanding of the complex problems facing the late Yi dynasty as it attempted to cope with numerous foreign and domestic crises.

Because the letters deal with such a wide range of activities, I have thought it helpful to divide them into four separate categories. The letters in each category have been placed in chronological order. The first section, "Denny's Personal Affairs," includes such topics as efforts to obtain household supplies, Denny's relations with other foreigners in Korea, and problems concerning Denny's salary. Topics in the second section, "International Diplomacy in Korea," range from the British occupation of Port Hamilton (Kŏmundo) to the dispatch of Korean representatives abroad. The third section deals primarily with the controversy caused by the 1888 publication of Denny's well-known pamphlet, *China and Korea*. The final section concerns Denny's attempts to develop Korea's economy and finances.

While these divisions may help to develop important themes within the volume, readers should keep in mind that many of the letters touch on a variety of topics, some of which remain outside even these broad categories. At least one other element should be taken into account when reading these letters. With a few exceptions, the letters were written as part of Denny's private correspondence. They were not meant for the public record. Consequently Denny often used rather blunt language, language he might have altered had he ever considered publishing these letters as a set.

Regarding the sources of the letters, Letter 25 comes from the Thomas F. Bayard Papers, Library of Congress, Washington, D.C. All other letters are taken from Owen Nickerson Denny's Letterbook, located in the Special Collections of the University of Oregon Library, Eugene, Oregon.

For the most part, the sentence structure, grammar, and spelling of the original letters have been retained. For example, Denny referred to the peninsular kingdom both as "Korea" and "Corea." He often added or dropped an "e" at the end of some words—and he almost always misspelled "refered." Thus there are apparent inconsistencies in some of the spellings—Peking and Tokyo, for instance, may appear as Pekin and Tokio. I have sometimes added paragraph headings and punctuation in order to clarify Denny's meaning. Occasionally ellipses have been used either to indicate irrelevant material left out or because certain words were illegible. The original letters were not numbered; I have added the numbers (that is, 1 through 46) to simplify references.

In addition to the letters, which serve as the focus of this volume, I have included two appendixes. Appendix A contains six articles published originally in Asian and American newspapers while Denny was in Korea. They are reprinted here for three specific purposes. First, they are related to Denny's letters. By reading these articles in conjunction with the letters, one gets a clearer picture of some of the problems Denny was confronting. At the same time, the articles also help to capture some of the flavor of that long-ago period. Finally, the articles themselves are now quite rare, often available to only a few scholars on hard-to-read microfilm. It is hoped that their inclusion here will broaden our general knowledge of Korean history.

Appendix B contains Denny's pamphlet, *China and Korea*, in its entirety. Denny's letters, as well as his whole career in Korea, cannot be properly understood without an examination of this valuable document. Moreover, the pamphlet has traditionally been viewed as an important English-language source for late Yi dynasty historiography. These two considerations, together with the rareness of the document, suggest that a reprinting of *China and Korea* is long overdue.

A few words about the photographs included in this book are in order. Almost all of them are reproduced here for the first time. As such, they are valuable historical records in their own right and should add significantly to our visual knowledge of nineteenth-century Korea. Unless otherwise noted, all photographs are courtesy of Mrs. Stephanie Scott Williams.

The development of this book would have been impossible without the help of several persons and organizations. I am especially indebted to Dr. Choe Young Hee, the former President of the Korean National History Compilation Committee, and to Mr. Shin Ji-hyun, the former Research Director of the same institute. Through their support, I was first given the opportunity of working with various Denny materials, an opportunity which ultimately resulted in the publication (1981) of a volume by the Korean National History Compilation Committee entitled *Denny munsŏ* (Owen N. Denny's Documents on Korea). Although this limited edition was not available for public purchase in either Korea or the United States, it helped to lay the groundwork for the present volume.

In addition, I wish to thank Dr. Kim Won-mo of Dankook University for his assistance and hospitality during my trips to Seoul in the summers of 1978 and 1980. Mr. William C. Ralston, grandnephew of Owen N. Denny, and Mrs. Stephanie Scott Williams, great-granddaughter of Mrs. Owen N. Denny, opened their homes and private family collections to me, for which I will be forever grateful. The late Mr. Martin Schmitt, Mr. Edward Kemp, and Mr. Kenneth W. Duckett—all with the University of Oregon Library's Special Collections—kindly provided access to Denny's letters held at that institution. The staff of the Oregon Historical Society, and in particular Mr. Louis Flannery, Chief Librarian of the Society, supplied valuable support at important stages of the project. I also wish to express my deep appreciation to Dr. Francis J. Kerins, President of Carroll College, Sr. Mary Sarah Fasenmyer, Vice-President for Academic Affairs at Carroll College, Fr. Clayton S. Meyer, Carroll's former Vice-President for

Academic Affairs, and Fr. Jeremiah T. Sullivan, Head of Carroll's History Department, for their aid and interest. I owe a special debt of thanks to my good friend, Jim Shon, who first suggested the preparation of this volume and then provided valuable support at a critical stage of the project.

Above all else, it is with the utmost affection that I once again acknowledge the crucial support I have received from my wife, Kyung-ok. Without her encouragement and sacrifices this book would have never been completed.

Robert R. Swartout, Jr.
Carroll College
Helena, Montana

An American Adviser
in Late Yi Korea

Korea, Late Nineteenth Century

Editor's Introduction

The last five decades of the Yi dynasty (1392–1910) proved to be one of the most turbulent periods in all of Korean history. During that time Korea changed from an isolated, Confucian-oriented country to one struggling to maintain its autonomy amid the harsh realities of both Western and Asian imperialism. And while this international competition over who might control the peninsula was developing—a competition which would ultimately lead to Tokyo's seizure of Korea in 1910 as a Japanese colony—domestic conflicts within the troubled kingdom were also increasing. King Kojong, ruler of Korea during most of these years, was often deeply involved in many of the critical problems of his nation.[1]

A controversial issue facing King Kojong during the early years of his rule, and one which was tied to both foreign and domestic considerations, was whether or not to open the country to foreign contacts. Kojong's father, the Taewŏn'gun (Yi Ha-ŭng), who had ruled the country as a de facto regent from 1864 to 1873 before the King came of age, had strongly opposed such contacts. In fact he had successfully thwarted both French (1866) and American (1871) attempts to penetrate Korea's self-imposed isolation with military force.[2]

Despite the short-term success of the Taewŏn'gun's foreign policy King Kojong, who took over the controls of government from his father by 1874, realized that it would be increasingly difficult to turn aside future foreign pressures to open the country. This realization was supported by recent developments in China, where opposition to Western advances during the middle nineteenth century had only led to one defeat after another for the Chinese. Japan, on the other hand, had pragmatically opened its doors to the West and thus seemed well on its way to great national strength and development.

A turning point in Korean history occurred in 1876 when Kojong and the Korean government accepted the Kanghwa Treaty with

Japan—the peninsular kingdom's first modern diplomatic agreement. To be sure, the Japanese, by sending a heavily armed naval fleet into Korean waters to support the signing of a treaty, did not give the Koreans many options. Nonetheless, the treaty was not simply the result of Japanese pressure. By 1876 Kojong and many of his reform-minded advisers had already decided that it was time for Korea to enter into modern diplomatic relations. Such relations would possibly allow Korea to stabilize, and perhaps even improve, its position in the rapidly changing world of international rivalries.[3]

As international rivalries increasingly focused on Korea in the late 1870s and early 1880s, Kojong began looking for other parties that might be willing to support Korean interests. One likely candidate appeared to be the United States. Among the various Western powers operating in East Asia, America seemed to be one of the least threatening to Korea. The United States had certainly taken advantage of the West's unequal treaties with China and Japan in order to expand its commercial activities in East Asia. Yet the Americans had not been inclined—as had the British and the French, for example—to seize Asian territories as colonial possessions. This Korean view of U.S. attitudes, coupled with America's traditional commercial interests in Korea,[4] eventually led to the signing of an 1882 Korean-American treaty, often called the Shufeldt treaty because of the role played by the American negotiator Robert W. Shufeldt.[5]

Kojong's hopes for American support of Korean interests appeared to be reinforced soon after the signing of the 1882 treaty. America's first diplomatic representatives in Korea, Lucius H. Foote and George C. Foulk, were enthusiastic advocates of Korean independence and development.[6] Indeed, with hardly an exception all the American ministers serving in Seoul between 1883 and 1905 strongly supported these policies.[7] In addition to the openly pro-Korean stance of America's official representatives in Seoul, the unofficial American community gathering in Korea after 1882—composed primarily of missionaries and businessmen—also pushed for a politically independent Korea.[8]

One important result of this budding Korean-American connection was King Kojong's request—in fact, several requests—for American advisers to serve the Korean government. These advisers would range from military instructors to agricultural experts; from diplomatic specialists to English-language teachers.[9] The purpose of employing such advisers was twofold. First, they would instruct Koreans in various technical, political, and economic fields, thereby helping to modernize Korea as it struggled to compete with the advanced nations. Second, it was hoped that by simply being Americans they could and would work to prevent the take-over of Korea by some other foreign power. This second factor was undoubtedly the major reason for Kojong's decision to employ Owen Denny as one of his principal foreign advisers.

The role of China in all these developments should be noted. Because of Korea's critical geographic location in Northeast Asia, the Chinese were vitally concerned about its security. If another major power were to seize the peninsula, it could then use that territory to threaten directly the homeland of the Ch'ing dynasty—Manchuria. This Chinese fear became more pronounced during the late nineteenth century as both Russian and Japanese power grew in Northeast Asia. China's concerns were such that the Middle Kingdom, and especially Viceroy Li Hung-chang, played a central role in arranging the 1882 Korean-American treaty. Li believed that America, and perhaps other Western nations as well, could be used in Korea to thwart apparent Japanese designs on the kingdom.[10] This Chinese involvement in Korean foreign affairs was soon matched by Peking's intervention in Korean domestic matters. During the Imo revolt of 1882 and the Kapsin coup of 1884 the Chinese sent troops and officials to Seoul to remove Korean officials who appeared to threaten China's policies in the peninsula. These actions, China's first direct interference in Korean domestic affairs since the Manchu invasions of the early seventeenth century, illustrated Peking's determination to prevent any changes in Korea that might weaken China's own national security.[11]

In addition to stationing troops in Korea, Li Hung-chang dispatched Yuan Shih-k'ai, whose name in the years ahead would become synonymous with Chinese oppression in the peninsula, to direct Chinese affairs. And since the Koreans were greatly interested in employing foreign, especially American, advisers, Li also took this opportunity to recommend to Kojong a personal friend of his—none other than Owen N. Denny. Li was sure that he could thus satisfy two needs simultaneously: Kojong would receive his much desired American adviser, and Li would have serving in Korea another official who, because of his relationship with the Chinese Viceroy, would presumably support China's interests there. Consequently, for two quite different reasons—Korea's interest in American aid and Chinese determination to control Korea—Owen Denny on April 9, 1886, received his joint appointment as Vice-President of the Korean Home Office and Director of Foreign Affairs.[12]

Owen Nickerson Denny was born on September 4, 1838, to Christian and Eliza Denny in Morgan County, Ohio. In 1852 he accompanied his parents and five brothers and sisters to the then territory of Oregon. Adopting Oregon as his new home, young Denny quickly began to prosper. A hard worker, he helped to pay his own way through first Lebanon Academy and then Willamette College in Salem. Following the completion of his formal education Denny chose to pursue a legal career. After studying law under lawyers in both Salem and Oregon City, he passed the state bar examination in 1862.[13]

Denny began his career in law by joining the staff of C. R. Meigs, then prosecuting attorney for Oregon's Fifth District (Oregon had become a state in 1859). Shortly thereafter he was appointed by Governor A. C. Gibbs to complete the term of a recently vacated judgeship in Wasco County. Although his term soon expired, Denny regained the position through election and served a four-year term until 1868. In December of that year he married Gertrude Hall White, who would be his constant companion and a source of great strength throughout his future years of service in both the United States and East Asia.[14]

In 1870 Denny was elected police court judge in Portland, "and forever after bore a judge's title as part of his name."[15] During these early years in Oregon he became an active member of the Republican Party. As a result of his party loyalty and his legal background, in 1874 President Ulysses S. Grant appointed him collector of internal revenue for Oregon and Alaska. The federal appointment was followed by an even more important one in 1877. In that year President Rutherford B. Hayes, Grant's successor, selected Denny to be United States consul at Tientsin, China.[16]

Denny accepted the Tientsin appointment on May 23, 1877, and was able to take over consulate affairs on September 20, 1877. Thus he began six years of service as an American consular official in China, years in which he would formulate many of his attitudes about Asia while developing a special and very important relationship with Li Hung-chang.

It was not too surprising that Denny and Li would become close friends during these years. Li's headquarters were in Tientsin, and therefore the two men would have many opportunities to meet. Even more important, both men were deeply interested in the modernization of China's transportation network, mining industry, and technology in general. Li was a frequent visitor at the Denny residence, where the two often discussed China's needs. It was during one of these visits that Denny reportedly remarked to Li: "Your Excellency, why do you send to these foreign countries for everything and pay such prices, when you have everything in your own country, and you have what other countries do not—cheap labor?"[17] Denny concluded that China should speed up its industrialization efforts so that it could compete effectively with other nations in international trade and commerce. These words would certainly have great appeal to the man who was often the leading spokesman for the Chinese Self-Strengthening Movement.[18]

As an indication of Denny's consular success in Tientsin, in the spring of 1880 he was appointed United States consul general at Shanghai. Among the American consular and diplomatic positions in China this one was second only to the minister's post at Peking in importance. During his three and a half years in Shanghai, Denny continued to support Chinese modernization and to cultivate Li Hung-chang's friendship. The two men got along so well that at one point Li recommended Denny be named United States minister to China.[19] Although this appointment never came about, the recommendation demonstrated the closeness of their relationship. Yet if Li thought this friendship could be used to control Denny's actions once the Judge began work in Korea, he was sadly mistaken. As a matter of fact, the affair which caused Denny to leave the American consular service, and thus made him available to accept the Korean position, could have provided Li with some inkling as to the Judge's future attitudes.

Between 1880 and 1883 a major conflict developed between Denny and George F. Seward, a former American consul general and minister to China. While serving as America's consul general in Shanghai (1863–75), Seward arranged for the personal construction of a consulate which he, as the actual owner, leased to subsequent United States government officials. This was the facility that Denny took over when he became consul general. Upon assuming the post, Denny soon discovered that Seward's rental charges for the consulate—Seward still controlled the lease—were exorbitant. He strongly believed that Seward was taking advantage of both the United States government and the occupant of the consulate (in the case, Denny himself) to line his own pockets. Consequently Denny recommended that the State Department void Seward's arrangement and give permission to construct a new consulate that would eliminate Seward's involvement. After over two years of almost constant fighting—in which, among other things, Seward filed suit against Denny in the Supreme Court of the District of Columbia—the State Department finally decided the issue in favor of Seward.[20] Denny of course could have swallowed his pride and continued with his respected position in Shanghai. This, however, he refused to do. He was convinced that he had to stand up for his own principles, and if that demanded his resignation from the consular service, then so be it. On October 9, 1883, Denny wrote to the State Department:

> It has been more than six years since I entered the Consular service in China during which time I have endeavored to serve the government faithfully and honestly and now in return for these services I am compelled to appeal from the partial and unwarrantable action of that Department from which I had a right to expect exact Justice at least; for rather than submit to such treatment I shall surrender the office which I hold and which I have not disgraced.[21]

Had Li Hung-chang taken closer notice of Denny's independent nature and the Judge's determination to stick to his principles during this affair, perhaps he would have been less surprised when his own attempts to dominate Denny in the years ahead failed.

Upon his April 1886 arrival in Seoul, Denny was faced with the task of getting himself settled in the Korean community. The financial arrangements of his original two-year contract were generous: he was to receive annually 12,000 taels ($15,360).[22] In addition to his salary he and Mrs. Denny needed a residence of their own. Fortunately for the Dennys the Korean government was willing and able to provide them with very suitable quarters. Their compound, which many foreign residents in Seoul referred to as the "Denny Palace," was composed of a large traditional Korean house, some smaller buildings, and an expansive courtyard, all enclosed by a high wall. After taking possession of these impressive facilities the Dennys proceeded to remodel much of their "palace" to suit their own Western needs and habits.[23] This in turn required the purchase of extensive supplies from abroad, for very few Western items were then available in Korea. As many of Denny's letters illustrate, even when these items were available from such ports as Shanghai, the problems of ordering, shipment, and payment were a constant source of frustration. Of course, the Dennys could have simplified their problems by living as the Koreans lived, but few Westerners residing in nineteenth-century East Asia were willing to do that. To people such as Owen Denny, the retention of American and European life-styles was not just a matter of convenience. These practices also seemed to exemplify the technological, if not cultural, superiority of Western civilization.

Even before Denny could finish putting his personal affairs in order, he found himself thrust into the thick of Korean politics. As he became increasingly involved in these political problems, two primary goals came to dominate his thinking. First, he became deeply committed to the policy of political independence for Korea. Second, he grew to believe that such independence could not be permanently achieved without the commercial and economic development of the peninsula. While these two aims came to determine many of his actions in Korea, they also served eventually to bring him into conflict with those Chinese officials who formulated Peking's Korean policy.

Denny was convinced, as was King Kojong, that if Korea was to become a truly independent nation, the kingdom had to conclude more international treaties with as many foreign powers as possible. One important step in this direction was the signing in June 1886 of a Franco-Korean treaty of amity and commerce, a tariff schedule, and regulations governing French trade in Korea. It is important to note that Denny not only played a vital role in negotiating these agreements, but also officially signed them on behalf of the Korean government.[24]

The Franco-Korean treaty of 1886 was not the only bilateral agreement that Denny helped to conclude for Korea. In August 1888 the Judge finally completed two years of often difficult negotiations with his personal friend Karl Waeber, then Russian chargé d'affaires in Seoul. The result of these efforts was the signing of a valuable commercial agreement between Korea and Russia that was designed to regulate trade along the Tumen River boundary. Although this agreement—like almost all Western treaties signed with East Asian nations in the nineteenth century—discriminated against Korea, it did help to bring peace and order to a traditionally troubled border area. Moreover, it tended to strengthen Korea's claims of independence, since it was assumed by many observers that only a sovereign nation could negotiate and sign such a treaty.[25]

In addition to these two bilateral treaties Denny also played a role in ending the British occupation of Kŏmundo (Port Hamilton). In April 1885 Great Britain's naval force had seized control of the islands that made up Kŏmundo as part of a larger strategy to block possible Russian expansion throughout Central and East Asia.[26] Upon arriving in Korea, Denny quickly came to oppose the British occupation. He advised Li Hung-chang that the British move only helped to increase the possibility of an eventual Anglo-Russian confrontation in Korea, and thus recommended that Great Britain withdraw immediately.[27] Following an oral promise by Russian officials in October 1886—a promise guaranteed by the Chinese— that St. Petersburg had no intention of occupying Kŏmundo, the British decided to return the port to Korean authority. Finally, on February 27, 1887, the last of Great Britain's naval forces were withdrawn from Port Hamilton.[28]

Although Denny's role in the above affair was no doubt limited, the same cannot be said for his involvement in the Korean decision to dispatch diplomatic representatives to the United States and Europe. Kojong himself had come to the conclusion in 1887 that the sending of such representatives was vital if Korea was to maintain its independence, an independence that was being increasingly threatened, not by Russian or Japanese encroachment, but rather by Chinese aggression. From the Chinese point of view the Koreans, and especially the King, were becoming more and more difficult to control. If Kojong were successful in establishing permanent missions abroad, his reluctance to follow China's policies and advice would be strengthened. Therefore Peking exerted extensive pressure on Kojong to cancel the proposed missions. Although the King was temporarily forced to compromise some of his goals for the envoys because of the Chinese pressure,[29] in the long run he fought to maintain the independence of, and his control over, such missions. And throughout this crisis Kojong received the constant and determined support of his American adviser. Thus, through the joint efforts of Denny and the King, Pak Chŏng-yang successfully left Korea during the winter of 1887–88 and became the peninsular kingdom's first permanent minister to the United States.[30]

As the issue of sending ministers abroad indicated, Denny believed that despite his ties with Li Hung-chang his first loyalty must be to his employer, the Korean government, and particularly to King Kojong. For this reason he opposed Chinese efforts to dominate Korean foreign and domestic affairs, and ultimately became one of the most outspoken critics of Peking's Korean policy. His distrust of Chinese intentions was reinforced by the aggressive actions of China's representative in Seoul, Yuan Shih-k'ai.[31] One result of the Judge's anti-Chinese position was the publication in 1888 of his *China and Korea*. In this pamphlet he strongly condemned Yuan's behavior in Korea; at the same time he presented a highly controversial legal argument for Korea's international status as an independent nation. Regarding the latter issue, Denny did admit that there were strong traditional ties between China and Korea, ties often based upon their common Confucian heritage. Yet notwithstanding this fact Denny maintained that a new diplomatic age had begun in East Asia, one which emphasized the primacy of Western international law. If Korea was to survive as a nation in this new legal and diplomatic environment, it would have to accept and use effectively these Western techniques. And in fact this was one of the major reasons for the employment of Denny as a Western adviser: to teach the Koreans the art of Western diplomacy.[32]

Of course, any political independence would mean little if Korea could not develop its commercial and economic potential, for Denny was convinced such development would have to serve as the basis for domestic stability and security. As early as February 1887 he began advocating the expanded development of mineral resources in P'yŏngan Province and the opening of P'yŏngyang as a major commercial center. Gradually Denny tied these two ideas to a larger economic program. According to this plan, an American group of bankers organized by Everett Frazar of New York City would loan the Korean government $2,250,000 to help relieve the kingdom's financial problems. In addition, Frazar's company was to be given special mining and railroad concessions in Korea that would help to modernize the country's economy while providing the Americans with a solid return on their investments. Ultimately it was the failure of the Korean government to approve this complex package that would cause Denny to leave Korea in anger and frustration.[33]

In evaluating Denny's overall performance in Korea, it is clear that, despite limited (albeit not unimportant) successes such as the 1886 Franco-Korean treaty and the 1888 Russo-Korean trade agreement, he failed to achieve his long-range goals of Korean political independence and economic development. The various reasons for this failure illustrate both the scope of the problems facing nineteenth-century Korea and the limitations under which Owen Denny operated.

Among the reasons for Denny's failure certainly one of the most important was Chinese opposition to his plans. As Denny increased his criticism of Chinese actions in the peninsula, Li Hung-chang and other Chinese officials unsuccessfully pressured King Kojong to terminate the American's contract. Following Denny's signing of a second two-year contract in the spring of 1888 the Chinese tried another approach. The Judge constantly had trouble collecting his salary, as many of his letters make clear, because of the financial chaos of the government.[34] The Chinese hoped to use this problem, as well as Denny's dislike for Yuan Shih-k'ai, to remove him. In December 1888 Chinese officials met with Denny in Shanghai and promised to pay his salary still outstanding (about 20,000 taels) and recall Yuan from Seoul if the Judge would leave Korea. Denny agreed to the arrangement on the condition that Kojong's consent be included and that he be allowed to return should the King invite him back. Basing his account on this agreement, the historian Hosea Morse in his much quoted study, *The International Relations of the Chinese Empire*, concluded that Denny "withdrew [from Korea], having with the best intentions and from the most loyal motives, wrought much mischief."[35]

Morse's statement is incorrect. Denny and his wife did take an extended vacation during the first months of 1889. But by the summer of that year they returned to Seoul, incensed that the Chinese had not lived up to their promise of recalling Yuan. Kojong, realizing that Denny was more than willing to return to his post, quickly arranged for the final payment of the American's first two-year contract. Denny then resumed his responsibilities and in fact completed all of his second two-year contract.[36] Yet if the Chinese were unsuccessful in removing Denny, they were capable of thwarting many of the Judge's plans for Korea. They often did this by supporting conservative Korean officials who disapproved of Kojong's reform measures and by intimidating others who might be inclined to go along with the King and Denny. Behind the scenes such tactics were undoubtedly used to persuade the Korean government to turn down Denny's detailed program for economic development. In the long run this proved critical, for the collapse of the economic negotiations on behalf of Frazar forced Denny to refuse Kojong's offer to sign a third two-year contract.[37]

Problems within Korea itself also greatly limited Denny's chance of success. The severe economic and financial weakness of the country made it extremely difficult for Korea to maintain its political independence. And this weakness was too often exacerbated by the power of the traditional Korean bureaucracy. Many Korean bureaucrats opposed not only the reforms of King Kojong and the progressives, but also the possible growth of the King's powers which lay behind some of the reform measures. As a person who was closely identified with the monarch's policies and programs, Denny was viewed with suspicion by many such government officials. Faced with this opposition, it is not surprising that Denny had a very difficult time of gaining support for his domestic programs.[38]

A third factor which inhibited Denny's ability to achieve his goals was the official position of the U.S. Department of State toward Korean independence. Between 1882 and 1905 the United States government consistently approved of Korean independence; yet at the same time it refused to give the kind of support—either in terms of troops, money, or a defense alliance—which would have guaranteed the continued sovereignty of the kingdom. This was primarily because American interests in China, and later in Japan, far outweighed those in Korea; thus, the United States was unwilling to anger the two larger Asian nations by providing direct support to Korea. Secretary of State Thomas F. Bayard's 1887 recall of George Foulk, a strong opponent of Chinese domination in Korea, was an important illustration of this American policy in practice.[39] Another example of this was Bayard's refusal in 1888 to permit Hugh A. Dinsmore to leave his position as United States minister to Korea in order to become the personal adviser of King Kojong. Bayard believed that such a change would compromise America's neutral policy toward Korea.[40] Had the Department of State been willing to support actively Korean independence, the influence of Denny and other Americans in Korea would have been much stronger.

One other reason for Denny's failure to achieve his goals in Korea was that, as an "intruder" from the West, he faced continual problems caused by differences of language and culture. Forced to rely upon sometimes inexpert Korean translators, Denny often was not sure if the true meaning of his words reached the King and other high officials. In addition, he undoubtedly had a difficult time comprehending the nature of Korean culture. Many Korean officials, on the other hand, may have resented the intrusion of this American into their midst and thus were probably disinclined to work closely with Denny. Consequently, although his titles of Vice-President of the Home Office and Director of Foreign Affairs implied positions of power, Denny's actual ability to influence the Korean decision-making process was greatly limited by these language and cultural differences. He was, after all, an official for Korea, not a Korean official.

And what about Owen Denny the individual? How might we evaluate his overall performance in Korea? There is no doubt that the King's adviser possessed some serious shortcomings. For instance, Denny's strong-willed personality often created problems for him with other officials, both Korean and foreign. His particular sense of right and wrong sometimes caused him to interpret opposing positions, including the foreign policies of other nations, as personal attacks upon himself. This interpretation, in turn, led to various responses, such as his determination to publish *China and Korea*, which in the short run further exacerbated his relationships with several key officials, including Li Hung-chang.[41]

Even more important than this issue of temperament was Denny's tendency to act as an agent of Western imperialism. By helping to negotiate and sign such pacts as the Franco-Korean treaty of 1886 and the Russo-Korean trade agreement of 1888, Denny was reinforcing the use of the "unequal treaty system" to secure special political benefits for Western powers in East Asia. Moreover, this form of political imperialism was augmented by a rather significant degree of economic imperialism. As the various letters in Part IV of this study clearly illustrate, Denny was a strong supporter of American commercial and financial penetration of Korea—a penetration which was designed to provide United States firms and businessmen with a number of valuable concessions.

In addition to these political and economic considerations Denny, like most Westerners of his day, was a rather firm believer in what might be called cultural imperialism. He was convinced that one of his major responsibilities in the peninsula was to transplant the benefits of "Western civilization" in Korean soil. This task would not be easy. To one of his close friends Denny once wrote that there could be no safe prediction "as to whether contact with western civilization will do anything towards getting them [the Koreans] out of the indolent groove they have been in for centuries past. Let us hope it will."[42] Obviously, if Korea was to move ahead culturally or economically, it was imperative that the kingdom adopt the Western—preferably the American—model.

Yet before we dismiss Owen Denny as simply another imperialist, we must take note of some of his special strengths. To begin with, it should be remembered that the Judge from Oregon practiced the art of politics during the Age of Imperialism. For him to possess none of the traits of that age would have been not only unusual but also illogical. Just as important as his Western biases is the fact that, by the standards of his own day, he was what might be labeled a "benevolent imperialist." That is, his brand of imperialism was without doubt considerably milder than that practiced by the great imperial powers of the late nineteenth century—Great Britain, France, Germany, and Russia. Even within the context of late Yi dynasty history Denny's efforts to "exploit" Korea appear rather benign when compared with the harsh realities of first Chinese and then Japanese aggression.

Finally, despite all of Denny's various problems and shortcomings, it would be wise to recall his principal long-range goals for Korea, goals which he remained committed to throughout his four trying years of service to the peninsular kingdom. Above all else Denny hoped to create a politically independent and economically prosperous Korea. While his methods of achieving these goals occasionally left something to be desired, the goals themselves are worth commendation—especially in an era of power politics. Too often during such periods the basic rights—including national freedom itself—of smaller nations have been trampled under by the political and military might of their larger neighbors. If those various officials who were responsible for formulating foreign policies concerning Northeast Asia had paid greater attention to the ideals of Owen Denny, then the history of twentieth-century Korea might have been much less tragic, and the lives of thousands of Koreans could have been far brighter.[43]

The Letters of
Owen Nickerson Denny

Part I.
Denny's Personal Affairs

Seoul, May 24, 1886

My dear Mr. Walsh,

I enclose a check on the Hong Kong and Shanghai Bank for the sum of Dollars 515, being the amount of my note and interest which you hold for money you so kindly advanced me while in Japan.[1] No doubt you wonder why you have not heard from me ere this, but the truth is I have been a very busy man ever since I left Shanghai and as a consequence my correspondence has been so much neglected that I hardly know which letter to answer first. When I arrived here I found business had accumulated considerably in the past six months awaiting me. This together with my efforts to get settled has kept me fully occupied. I like the situation assigned me by His Majesty for a residence very much. We shall be very comfortable.[2] Mrs. Denny arrives from Shanghai by the Tsugura Maru from Chefoo on the 2nd of June with furniture, stores &c, by which time our house will be ready. So far I am agreeably impressed with the prospect of accomplishing some good results. Just now I am engaged with the French Treaty. The first meeting of the convention takes place today at the Foreign Office.[3] Please let me hear from you.

Sincerely yours,
O. N. Denny

Seoul, June 20, 1886

Dear Mr. Wetmore,[4]

Your welcome favor of the 10th instant is just at hand. We were both delighted to learn of your safe return and that the trip had toned you up for the most trying part of the Shanghai climate. I wish you could have given us a call on your way back. You must come and make us a visit in Sept. when it is delightful. Now it is raining almost all the time. We are now comfortable in our new house and quarters. Not withstanding this, and the fact that I am the recipient of a good salary, yet it will be hard for me to stay unless I can accomplish some good for these people. This is the problem now to be solved. . . . Things have been very quiet here ever since I came, but how long they will stay so is hard to tell. I hope, however, that it is not "the calm before the storm." There are lots of cliques here, each trying to defeat the acts of the other. The problem of independent government is certainly yet unsolved. Neither can any safe prediction be made as to whether contact with western civilization will do anything towards getting them out of the indolent groove they have been in for centuries past. Let us hope it will. I enclose you a check for the sum of $39.21, the balance of your account, with cordial thanks for all the trouble you have taken to serve me. Please write me when you have leisure. I should have written you sooner, but I have been literally driven to death and my correspondence has been sadly neglected. We join in assurances of friendship and esteem for Mrs. Wetmore and yourself.

Sincerely yours,
O. N. Denny

LETTER 3

Seoul, July 13th, 1886

My dear Mr. Wetmore,

I have been rather expecting a letter from you the past eight or ten days. Hope your business is so well that you have not been able to write to me. We enjoyed Mrs. Wetmore's own letter to Mrs. Denny, which she will reply to soon. I enclose a check on the H.K. & S. Bank for $4.80. I have been very busy ever since I came here from Shanghai—concerned mostly with Mollendorff's blunders and don't know when I shall be through with them.[5] We were sorry to hear that you were ill after your return from Japan. Hope you are all right now. If you had come via Seoul and visited us last month I am sure you would have gone through the heat of Shanghai with "flying colors." This climate is far ahead of any other port in the East that we know of. The summer months' nights are cool; even the days are not as trying as they are in Shanghai. The nights are so cool that you always feel good in the morning and ready for the business of the day.

I used to think that procrastination always ruled the hour in China, but if you multiply it by twenty you will come near getting the result [in Korea]. And although I am always busy, yet the result is not satisfactory. Perhaps coming from a land full of progression, brains [?] and inoculive [sic] genius, where everything goes at rails and lightning speed, makes me impatient and in a measure unfits me for the surroundings where a "snails gallop" is swiftness in comparison (this for Mrs. Wetmore). I fully sympathize with the King, for he is broad and progressive, but he is almost alone. I hope I shall be able to help him.

We have some splendid coal upon the Tatong [Taedong] River, about 130 miles from Chemulpo. . . . I shall try and go up to examine it. Should we work it, we shall have to either grant a concession or negociate a loan with which to open it. If a concession is granted, [I] shall submit the matter to you first. . . .

Mrs. Denny joins me in best compliments to you both.

Sincerely yours,
O. N. Denny

LETTER 4

Seoul, Nov. 1st, 1886

Dear Mr. Brown,[6]

The violin has not yet made its appearance, but will come *fiddling* along soon no doubt. Enclosed I check you on Shanghai as per your request for the sum of $26.48, the price of the outfit which you were so good as to pay for me. Mrs. D as well as the "judicial mind" thank you sincerely for all the trouble we have given you in this and other matters, and especially do we thank you for contributing so liberally and cordially to our comfort and pleasure during our recent visit to Tientsin. . . .

Admiral and Miss Shufeldt are our guests here.[7] They expect to stay for the winter as the King has ordered a house to be made comfortable for them, and when the spring time comes they purpose to go to China and on to the south where the power and influence of the Empire abound. Our house is now assuming very comfortable proportions for the winter, and if conspirators will let us alone we may be happy yet. Mrs. D joins me in kindest regards to you.

Sincerely yours,
O. N. Denny

LETTER 5

Seoul, Corea
July 20th, 1887

Rev. F. F. Ellinwood, D.D.
23 Center Street
New York City, U.S.A.

My dear Sir,

It is seldom that I notice reports put in circulation about my private or official character, for as a rule, these are well known and speak for themselves. But whenever it has seemed necessary, in order to protect my name or conduct from aspersions put upon one or both, I have not hesitated to do so.

I am informed that in August last a report was received by your Board here from you in which you refered to me as follows: "It is a pity about Judge Denny," or words of similar import. Now what I desire to know, Dr., is what were the reports and by whome reported that caused this reference, if it is true that it was so made. I make this request in order that I may have an opportunity of placing myself right in the eyes of one whose good opinion I esteem as highly as I do your own. If I had the time I should allude to some of the obstacles which surround the difficult position I am conscientiously trying to fill, but as I have not, I must wait until I have the pleasure of seeing you in person.

I am my dear Dr.,
yours faithfully,
O. N. Denny

LETTER 6

Seoul, Corea, Nov. 16th, 1887

Dr. F. F. Ellinwood
   Secty, Presbyterian Board
    Foreign Missions
     New York City

My dear Sir,

I thank you very much for your favor of the 8th of Sept., in response to my inquiry. While your explanation is entirely satisfactory, I desire to relieve your mind of any impression now resting upon it that your reference to me has been "twisted into an unfavorable reference to myself," for such is not the case. Since I came to Corea I have been vehemently assailed by all those who had political or other designs upon this little country because I have opposed them with all the force at my command. And about the time your letter to the Board arrived, the opposition seemed to be hottest. Naturally, such a reference to me at such a time—unexplained—would & did cause some wonder or speculation on the part of those who saw it as to its meaning. Such was the case with Dr. Heron & Mr. Underwood, two conscientious Christian gentlemen friends of mine, and who have supported me as warmly as they could since I came here, and whom I shall support in turn whenever opportunity offers.[8] Dr. Allen too is a friend of mine and has had my confidence to that degree that he was my physician up to the time of his departure. It was carelessness on his part, though, in not explaining to his colleagues the reference in your letter to me.[9]

Sincerely yours,
O. N. Denny

Seoul, Corea
Jan. 7th, 1888

J. McCracken, Esq.
Portland, Oregon

My dear Sir,

Your favor of Oct. 1st last, enclosed with your bill of $240 for 24 months storage of household goods, reached me by the mail before the last. I have written DeLashmutt to pay it.[10] I sincerely thank you for the kind wishes contained in your letter. My health, however, has not been as good for the past six months as I could wish, owing perhaps to the trying duties of the post I am endeavoring to fill. Although never more comfortably located then now, yet I have wished many times to quit the King's service and return to my webfoot home. The political condition of the kingdom has been much disturbed ever since I came, owing to China's apparent determination to abort its independence—a scheme I have of course opposed with all the energy I possessed. This opposition has added much to my responsibilities as well as anxiety. For some of the details of a life in Corea I must await a more opportune moment to give you. Please give my assurance of esteem and friendship to your good father, and believe me,

Sincerely yours,
O. N. Denny

LETTER 8

Seoul, Korea
June 6th, 1888

His Excellency
Chou Fu[11]
Tientsin, China

My dear Taotai,

I have delayed from time to time answering your kind letter in reference to the loan you made to me through Mr. Detring in the hope that I might be able to say just when I could repay you, and now that the moment has arrived, I hasten to write you. I am glad to learn that you are now enjoying good health and hope you have been well since I last saw you. I regret, however, more than I can express in a letter, that, on account of circumstances over which I had no controll, you should have been denied the use of the money loaned to me for such a long time, but sincerely hope it has not caused you too much inconvenience in the meanwhile.

On yesterday I received sufficient money to repay you. Immediately I wrote Mr. Tong, Secty. of your Legation in Seoul, informing him of the fact and that I desired to pay the principal of Taels 2000, together with 8 percent interest; [and asking] would he receive these sums or should I transmit the same direct to you. After communicating with you by wire, he informed me that you desired me to pay the principal to him, but as the loan was on friendly terms, you declined to receive any interest at all. Mr. Tong therefore would receive only the principal from me, which I paid him on yesterday. At the same time I informed him that I should write to you on the subject of interest—and upon this point, my dear Taotai, as I have had the use of the money far beyond the limit which intimate friendship could claim, I fear injustice may be done you if you adhere to your expressed purpose not to accept a reasonable amount of interest for the use of the money & which has accommodated me so much. I therefore beg you to give this matter further consideration, again thanking you most cordially for your favor to me, and expressing the hope that long life, honor and abundant prosperity may attend you.[12]

I am very sincerely yours,
O. N. Denny

LETTER 9

Seoul, Korea
Feb. 17th, 1889

My dear Mr. Dinsmore,[13]

In replying to the request contained in your favor of today, I have to say that on the 13th instant Major John G. Lee called at my office with a copy of the S. F. [San Francisco] *Examiner* in which he was criticised for having—as was alleged—among other things, read or examined some of the despatches of the Legation while

enjoying your hospitality.[14] After calling my attention to this partic-
ular charge, the Major said that Col. Long, Secretary of your
Legation,[15] had told him that you had made the charge to him
(Long) and that you had given me as your authority. I replied to
Major Lee that you could not and would not say that you told Col.
Long any such thing, because there was not a word of truth in it,
and thereupon proposed to accompany Major Lee to see you on
the matter.

The next morning, however, I called at the Legation, where I
informed you of my conversation with Major Lee of the day
previous, where you promptly pronounced the statement to be
untrue, just as I was sure you would do. You then asked me to call
with you at the office to see Col. Long, which I did, and when in
the Col.'s presence you informed him of the statements made to
me by Major Lee. The Col. said, "yes, I understood you to say that
Judge Denny was your authority." You replied, "Col. you are
mistaken. Judge Denny is not my authority, and I never could
have possibly told you that he was. Not only so, but I have good
reason to believe that all Judge Denny knows about the affair I told
him my-self," which is true. Col. Long still contended that he
understood you to give me as your authority, when you re-iterated
your denial, adding that you did not give anyone as your authority
at the time, but was quite prepared to do so when the proper time
came. You also conceded to the Col. good faith in the matter of his
contention, and said that he may have gotten his impression from
the mention of my name at some stage of the conversation,
although you had no recollection that it was mentioned at all.

You then proceeded to recall the principal feature of your
conversation with the Col., with a view, as I understood it, of
removing from his mind the wrong impression under which, as you
insisted, he was laboring. During this conversation the Col. said
that while he had never seen Major Lee reading the despatches of
the Legation, he (Col.) had seen him looking over some papers
lying on the table one day when he was in the office, and that upon
being reminded that that was not a proper thing to do, the Major
replied, "Oh, that does not matter as I read all the despatches in
Washington." Col. Long replied substantially that what he read in
Washington did not at all concern him; but what he saw here did
concern him very much as he was the custodian of the archives of

the Legation and responsible for their safe keeping.

We then left the office and entered the residence part of the Legation. Soon thereafter Col. Long also entered for the purpose, as he stated, of re-affirming his conviction that you had given him my name as your author, but which you again most positively denied. The Colonel while there again repeated that he had never seen Major Lee reading the despatches of the Legation; that the only thing he had seen the Major do was to look over some papers lying on the table in the office, as before stated, and for which he rebuked him. The above are the principal points of the conversation as I now recall them.

Sincerely yours,
O. N. Denny

LETTER 10

Seoul, July 21st, 1889

Dear General,[16]

I have just settled my salary account with the Korean government, and as a matter of course remain in the service of the King for at least eight months more, the balance of my second term. The government have paid me Tls. 20,000, the amount due on the first contract, and have given me a note under the seal of the Home Office for 10,000 payable in four months from this date. They have paid me interest on the accounts due. As the Chinese have acted very badly in not keeping the arrangement made last winter, I am going to remain in Korea, in which case I agreed to return the Taotai's checks, papers, &c. given in payment of my salary due from the Korean government, he [Taotai Kung] agreeing in that event to return my salary or check which included the Treasury Certificate given me by the Korean government. Will you please return to me by registered post the large package in the Chinese envelop, addressed to H.E. Taotai Kung, which contains my papers, and hand over to the Taotai the smaller package in the foreign envelop, addressed "O. N. Denny, Esq., Nagasaki, Japan," which contains the Taotai's papers. I thought it better to write you . . . and thereby guard against any mistake, as the matter is a most important one to me. Should H.E. the Taotai make an objection to this disposition of the packages placed in your hands by mutual agreement for final disposition, call his attention to our stipulation as recited on the first page of this letter, which should forever silence him. . . ."[17]

General, I regret exceedingly that the time of your departure seems so near at hand. It is one of those mistakes that our government seems to be making far too often for the effectiveness of the service, but wherever you are or whatever you may be engaged in, you can rest assured that the earnest prayers of Mrs. Denny and myself will go with you for your triumph in life. We do not expect to remain in the East any longer than it takes to wind up my affairs after the expiration of my contract, when we shall look forward with great pleasure to meeting Mrs. Kennedy and yourself on the other side.

I am going to further add to my debt of gratitude to you by asking you whenever opportunity offers to explain as far as you think advisable . . . the recent events with reference to myself and the Korean "question," as you know it so well. . . . Mr. Wetmore, as you remember, has a copy of the agreement made with the Chinese. Before leaving Shanghai I read it to both Mr. Little and others now of the *Mercury* [a Shanghai newspaper].

I have been very busy since my return with the affairs of the government, some of which got into a nice muddle while I was absent. I may mention 1st that a Korean servant of the French Consul, DePlancy, committed the unpardonable offense—according to Korean custom—of getting upon the wall and looking into the house of an official. The official caught & whipped the servant, whereupon the foolish Consul sent out the soldiers, which the King sent to protect the Consul's carcass, and arrested the official & took him into the Consulate & whipped him without saying any thing to the Korean Foreign Office about it. Then the Foreign Office demanded the servant to be delivered up, as provided by international usage as well as law, which the Consul refused to do, saying that he "proposed to teach these Koreans a lesson." The absurd and high-handed conduct of the Consul ought to get him in hot water.[18]

Then again, through Dr. Allen in Washington Korea is saddled with the biggest ignoramus of an "American mining expert"—so called—that ever afflicted any country. This so called expert, whose name is Pierce, without any proper examination of the quartz ledges of the country, selected a place which some one doubtless told him would be a good place to mine, and without a stroke of work in the way of development to see whether there was quality and quantity of ores which would justify further outlay in dollars—which every prudent man, whether miner or expert, always takes. But not so with Mr. Pierce; he rushes off and induces the King to let him telegraph to Allen to send over a complete ten stamp mill costing $15,000, as well as machinist and assistant. But Pierce's cable was so bunglingly worded that Allen mistook its purport and, instead of wiring back to know its meaning, proceeded to place his own interpretation as to Pierce's meaning & acted accordingly. Pierce telegraphed, "send ten stamp mill, machinist and for assistant John Stinner." Naturally enough, this made no sense to Allen, he thinking that Pierce wanted a machinist and *four* assistants. So Allen engaged *five* men instead of two, and all for one year, one at a monthly salary of $250, and the other four at $200 each per month.[19]

So we now have upon our hands a quartz mill and five miners, headed by a stupid man for an expert, all to do nothing except to worry over the payment of their salaries. The poor miners are not to blame. In fact, I feel sorry for them as they are chagrined and humiliated, besides all leaving good positions to come. Allen says in his letter that *all* of these four men are engaged as *foremen*. Just think of one quartz mill which will not do a lick of work in a year, if ever, having "four foremen." Usually for one small enterprise, *one* is ample. Allen further says that the "American expert" reports to him that the quartz is fabulously rich in gold; while Pierce in his reports to the government here says that the highest assay he has yet had is "fifty two Dollars" silver (in value) to the ton, where when you come to make a practice test may mean absolutely nothing at all (in case the ore is rebellious). The King has instructed me to try and arrange to send the 3 men not ordered back on the best terms that can be made, which I am now at work on. Perhaps one of the strangest features of this transaction is that Allen should do it through old Shufeldt. Allen is not so much at fault in not being able to understand the stupid. . . . [The remainder of this letter is not contained in Denny's letterbook.]

Seoul, Oct. 6th, 1889

General Han Kiu Sul[20]

My dear Sir:

You remember that more than eighteen months ago, when my first term of service was about to expire, I notified His Majesty that as my salary had not been paid as agreed and as His Majesty seemed unable to profit much from my advice, that I should leave Korea at the end of my contract. This the King begged me not to do, as you informed me many times, but asked me to continue in His Majesty's service by renewing my contract for another two years. If I would do so, the amount due, Taels 20,000, on the first contract should be paid as soon as the money from the sale of red ginseng arrived from China, which would be in about two months, and my salary for the future be paid each and every month out of the customs revenues. Relying upon this promise, and as His Majesty pressed me so hard to stay, saying if I did not it would look to foreigners as well as Koreans that I had no sympathy either for His Majesty or the government, I not only renewed my contract for two years more but in consideration of the above conditions being kept by the government, I of my own motion agreed to accept as salary $1,000 per month instead of taels 1,000 as under the first contract,[21] the President of the Foreign Office having said to me that the last named amount was too much.

I not only told you at the time the second contract was made that if its terms were not complied with the salary account would run in Taels as [compensation], but many times since. And as the government has failed and still fails to keep their stipulation with me in this regard, there is not a particle of consideration for the reduction. You will further remember that while I was in Nagasaki a few months ago, His Majesty telegraphed me that my account for salary would be paid upon my arrival here and asked me to return on important business. In response to this I returned by first steamer and shortly thereafter made up my account, which was not disputed except the charge of taels for fourteen months of the second contract. The government contended, that not withstanding their utter failure to keep their agreements with me which were the basis of the reduction, that I should accept dollars and not taels, which seemed to me to be both unfair and unjust; while I insisted that I should be paid in Taels up to the 1st of Aug. of the second contract, while the remaining eight months could be paid in Dollars if paid over in pursuance with the terms of the agreement. Otherwise, that sum would be demanded in Taels also. But as the government seemed to insist on their view, and as His Majesty proposed, if I would yield, to send me promptly taels 20,000 due on first contract and to settle in four months all then due on the second and the remainder as it became due, and as I wished to have the disagreeable matter settled as quickly as possible, I accepted the King's proposal. And although this was nearly three months ago, not one dollar has yet been paid me on account of salary due.

You will remember that His Majesty sent me checks for the Taels 20,000 on a Chinaman who dishonored them by refusing payment, when at your request I returned them to His Majesty through you. I write you now to inform you that as this second settlement has been entirely ignored by the government, I shall insist upon the salary under the second agreement being paid in taels up to Nov. 1st. The balance may be paid in dollars if paid as the same falls due, otherwise to be paid in taels also. I have also to add that unless these accounts are soon settled, I shall, as much as I regret to do so, be compelled to lay it before the United States Minister, and through the U.S. Legation, to the Hon. Secretary of State for the United States at Washington, as I am at a loss to understand why I am treated so badly after serving the King and government so faithfully.

Sincerely yours,
O. N. Denny

LETTER 12

Seoul, Feb. 17th, 1890

H. M. Bevin, Esq.
  Sub Manager
    Hong Kong & Shanghai Bank
    Shanghai

Dear Sir:

I thank you for your cordial letter of Jan. 31st just to hand. I am quite sure now that the receipts to which you allude cover Tls

30,000 which were *intended* to be paid to my credit by the Korean government on account of salary due & unpaid, as a few days after my letter to you of the 14th of Jan. a Korean who had been sent to Shanghai without my knowledge to arrange the business returned and delivered to me the receipts refered to in a manner that convinced me that *he* thought the money was already placed to my credit. And when I explained to him that the receipts were *not transferable* and that no one could draw the money except Chang Man, he seemed quite crest fallen. He then asked me to give him a letter to the Manager of your Bank, which I did. In my letter to Mr. Walter I detailed the circumstances as I then understood them and requested him as a favor to me to do what he could, not inconsistent with his official duties, to straighten out the muddle. The letter was sealed and contained the receipts refered to, and was addressed to Mr. Walter and handed to the Korean, who was to return to Shanghai and deliver it to the Manager in person, and who was to have left on the last *Tsuruga Maru* and should have been in Shanghai ere this. I thank you sincerely for your kind offer of assistance in this matter, and feel sure that with it the money will be passed to my account.

Yours faithfully,
O. N. Denny

LETTER 13

Seoul, April 8th, 1890

H. M. Bevin, Esq.
   Sub Manager
      Hong Kong & Shanghai Bank
      Shanghai

Dear Sir:

   I received some time ago your favor of Feb. 22nd informing me that Ta[e]ls 30,000 had been deposited to the credit of my account, and confirming your wire to same effect, which after deducting debits left a balance to my credit of Tls 29,253.21. The sum to have been deposited by the government was Tls 33,000. I of course upon receiving your letter asked the government why this had not been done. A few days ago the government informed me that they had received a telegram from the Korean who is in Shanghai, and who had been sent there to manage this business, saying that the balance of Tales [*sic*] 3,000 had been deposited to credit of my account. I replied that there must be some mistake about this, as the Bank has not so informed me. They then asked me to telegraph you, which I did two days ago by asking, "any additional deposit," but as yet no answer. I am quite certain there is none, but the government seemed to be in doubt, hence my wire. Should any be made at any time please wire me arrived.

Yours faithfully,
O. N. Denny

LETTER 14

Seoul, Nov. 4th, 1890

Hon. Van B. DeLashmutt
  Portland, Ogn.

My dear Van,

Your favor of Sept. 25th, with enclosure, just received. The situation with reference to my Arlington [Oregon] interests seems to be complicated enough. I hope you have not permitted anything to be done there which will in any way compromise my claim on the R.R. Co. for the money I have paid them. . . . It seems to me that any effort to get title to the land, except through the Co., is not only adding further complications, but is a hazardous one for me. However, I know you will do what you think is best for my interests.[22]

I regret now still more that I could not get away from this country last spring. I *hope* to do so between this and March next. In the meantime if you will be so good as to keep my life insurance, taxes & storage bill for furniture paid up I shall be under obligations to you. I shall send a check before long to square my account with you.

Very sincerely yours,
O. N. Denny

Part II.

International Diplomacy in Korea

LETTER 15

Seoul, Corea, June 29th, 1886

To His Excellency,
    Li Chung Tang,[23]
    Grand Secretary, Guardian of the
    Heir Apparent, Keeper of the Great Seal,
    Supt. of Trade for the Northern District,
    and Viceroy of the Province of Chihli

My dear Viceroy,
    Inclosed please find . . . a copy of a private and confidential letter addressed to me by a high Russian official which clearly portrays the Russian mind on the situation [the British occupation of Port Hamilton], and makes it apparent that only prompt action on the part of the British government will prevent further complications for both China and Corea. As I stated to your Excellency while last in Tientsin, in my judgment, there is no danger at all of any other nation occupying Port Hamilton [that is, Kŏmundo] in the event of the withdrawal of the English. Such an idea is advanced only as a pretext to continue in possession. Russia does not want Hamilton, but does want Lazareff [Yŏnghŭnghang], and if the British continue to hold the former, Russia will make the precedent an excuse for taking similar possession of the latter. England must know that China is determined to protect Corean territory from unfriendly occupation by other nations. And if she wishes to retain the friendship of your Excellency's great country, as well as to pursue a just course towards Corea, why does she continue a policy that is sure to result in giving both much additional trouble and concerne. So long as I remain here I shall do all I can to advance the interests of Corea, which will at the same time advance the interests of China, and to this end I earnestly beg

the aid of your wise and generous advice. I regret that I have not heard from you either directly or indirectly since my return.[24]

As ever your friend,
O. N. Denny

[Enclosure]

Private and Confidential

June 12th, 1886

Hon. O. N. Denny
Seoul

Dear Sir:

In justice to the government you are serving I feel it to be my duty to admonish you that if England continues much longer to hold temporary occupation of Port Hamilton, in my own opinion the Russian Government in self defense will be compelled to follow her example and take "temporary possession" of Port Lazereff, for the possession of this port is of as much importance, to say the least, to Russia as the other one is to England. Neither can the Corean government rightfully complain of our occupation of it so long as Hamilton is in the hands of the British government. In other words Russia ought not to be blamed if she follows the example set by so *great* and *just* a nation as England. Here I may add that for Russia the occupation of Port Lazereff by any other power would surely be more alarming and offensive than the possession of Port Hamilton by the same power could possibly be to England. The difference is this, while Port Hamilton in the hands of the English gives that nation the means only to *threaten* other people, yet if Lazereff were to fall into the hands of strangers, and especially if the strangers were jealous of Russia, it would amount almost to an invasion of our country. It is frankly admitted, I believe, by all Englishmen, that the occupation of Hamilton is an act of aggression on the part of the British government. . . . I am not prepared to say at this moment that it is a part of Russia's *settled* policy to take temporary possession of Lazereff, but I do say that if our press and people take up the matter and compell the Russian government to do so, it will be the fault of England alone.

[unsigned][25]

LETTER 16

Seoul, Aug. 12th, 1886

Dear Detring,[26]

I received a few days ago your long and welcome favor of the 29th of July, and by the same mail yours of the 30th, same month, enclosing code.[27] Both [came] through the hand of Merrill,[28] and found me in bed quite sick with a severe billious attack which came on about fifteen days ago. I am better now, but still weak and unfit for work.

In reply to your inquiry as to aca's[29] demand or request upon the Russians, I telegraphed you as follows: "I am assured aca made no such request—would be height of folly to do so & would violate agreement already made, [thus] involving serious trouble with China, in which event Russia must aid Corea, and since Port H[amilton] would be primary cause, British must support China. In the end the only real sufferer would be Corea. Besides even if no trouble arose, Corea would gain absolutely nothing beyond what she has by present arrangement; with Port H surrendered and Port L[azereff] left alone Corea has all protection she wants. This rumor doubtless is started as another lame excuse to retain Port H [by the British]. This view of the case I have laid before aca."[30]

The assurances I had of the falsity of the rumor came positively & from both sides. Now either Yuan[31] evolved it out of his reckless brain, or it arose out of the Hamilton business. At all events it is another one of those canards which Yuan telegraphs to the Viceroy about every other day. Two days ago I came in possession of some further news as to Russia's intuitions concerning Port L, and on yesterday wired you as follows: "Say to the Viceroy that it is absolutely necessary that the English without delay depart from

Hamilton or give some assurance that they will, as it is the only remedy for trouble with Russia over Lazereff. Besides it is the surest way to convince all that the Chinese are determined to maintain Corean dependency, which will make the Chinese stronger here."

I hope the Viceroy will lose no time in pressing the English to take this course as it is the only one to save a lot more complications over the Corean problem. The very air here, as well as the soil, seems to breed plots & counter-plots, with treason and murder in the leading role and all for the spoils that the possession of the offices gives. Even today I had unfolded to me from the very bowels of secrecy a deep laid scheme to carry off both the King & Queen and enthrone the Father [the Taewŏn'gun] instead, and that this is China's program as Yuan is *deep* in it. Such a scheme if attempted would cause the slaughter of all foreigners here and fill Corea with consternation and sorrow. In a few days I shall write you again on this subject, upon a full investigation of the rumor. I am quite sure however that there is some sentiment in the "wind" of some kind or other. Hope it is not of such a serious or desperate character as the above.[32]

Sincerely yours,
O. N. Denny

LETTER 17

Seoul, October 14th, 1886

Dear Detring,

We reached home all right. Had a delightfully smoothe passage.[33] Saw His Majesty the next day and explained the situation to him, and how near he came to total annihilation. The King seemed greatly relieved when I gave him the Chung tang's [Li Hung-chang's] assurances. He also seemed delighted with my visit to Tientsin as quite a change is noticable in Yuan's conduct here. His Majesty directed me to thank the Viceroy sincerely. So I sent the following telegram yesterday: "Message of Li Chung tang has been delivered to Corean King. Denny reported the critical situation and that Korean King was saved by the intervention of the Viceroy. I explained the basis of settlement which delighted the King who directed me to express profound gratitude to the Viceroy and to assure him of loyalty at all times."[34]

I am very busy and must cut my letter short this time. Keep me posted. I have not seen the gay . . . Yuan. I am told he is "sick & cannot go home."

Kindest regards Mrs. Detring & the family, in which Mrs. Denny heartily joins. As ever your friend,

Denny

LETTER 18

His Corean Majesty's Home Office
Seoul, Oct. 18th, 1886

To
   The Directors of the
     Nippon Yusen Kaisha
      Steam Ship Company
      Tokio, Japan

Gentlemen:
    Reports have reached His Majesty coming from an employee of your Company, it is said, as well as from other sources to the effect that the small steamer "Shima Maru," recently contracted for by the Corean government, was offered for sale by your Co. at Dollars 10,000. In view of this I have been instructed by His Majesty to inquire of your management what truth if any there is in these reports, to the end that injustice may not be done to the good name of the gentlemen who negociated the sale of the steamer or to the interests of the Corean government.[35]

        Very Respectfully,
        O. N. Denny
        Vice President of the Home Office

LETTER 19

Seoul, Nov. 1st, 1886

Dear Mr. Jansen,

I am just in receipt of your duplicate bill for $80.40. The original one I never saw or received, which will account for my delay in sending check, which I now do in H.K. & S.B. [Hong Kong and Shanghai Bank] for the amount as rendered. At this moment everything is very quiet, but how long it will stay so no man can tell, as the very air seems to breed conspiracies and intrigue. Recently China came very near putting her foot in it badly, in my judgment, in her attempted policy of annexing Corea. I am now very busy with the Russian overland trade regulations.[36] Hope your business is very prosperous.

Sincerely yours,
O. N. Denny

LETTER 20

Seoul, Corea
November 14th, 1886

Dear Mr. Frazar,[37]

Your very welcome letter of Aug. 13th, with press copy of yours of the 3rd of the same month enclosed, was handed me a few days ago by the President of the F.O. [Foreign Office] when there on business. I have not yet received the original of the Aug. 3rd letter. You should soon receive another letter from me, as I wrote you soon after my return from Tientsin where I went on a most important mission. I have never been so overwhelmed with work in my life as I have been for the last four or five months. The truth is it has been and is now a doubtful question as to whether or not the autonomy of this little kingdom, which is now struggling so heroically to get a foot hold on the great plains of western civilization, shall be preserved or not from the great land pirates which are menacing her now and have been for the past three years: England, which stands at the head, then Russia and last China.

England two years ago took possession of Port Hamilton against the repeated protests of Corea, and since then has been urging China to wipe out the government of Chosen and annex its territory to that of China. Of course she could not do this without some excuse, and the Chinese Representative here set to work to furnish such an excuse. He accused the King with writing a letter over the great seal inviting Russian protection, and undertook to furnish the proofs and in doing so showed up a most bungling piece of forgery. Either he was the author of it or was most stupidly imposed upon. Fortunately I discovered the plot in time to prevent any serious results to Corea, but not until 10 Chinese men of war had come to Chemulpo, and 3000 troops ordered to be in readiness to leave Port Arthur & 10,000 on the border between China and Corea. *But I stopped the mischief* any how for the present.

On the 3rd of Sept I left for Tientsin, taking Mrs. Denny with me, to protest to Li Chung Tang against the [acts] perpetrated on Corea, and to point out the serious trouble China came near getting into over the reckless conduct of her rash representative, as I know it would have been a war for China as Japan and Russia never would consent to anything like that. While neither of them in my judgment wants Corea, yet they don't intend that any one else shall take the peninsula. I laid the high handed and outrageous course of the Chinese minister or Consul [Yuan] rather fully and forcibly before the Viceroy. The past, I said, cannot be recalled, but we can prevent a recurrence of such things in the future by the adoption of the right kind of measures. [The discussion] was long and animated. I did not know but what it would result in straining our long friendly relations, but it turned out all right and we parted as good friends apparently as before. For the future, I suggested one of the following conditions as the basis of settlement: 1st, that all the treaty nations guarantee the integrity of Corea; 2nd, the three nations now chiefly interested in the kingdom [make the guarantee]; and 3rd, China and Russia do so. His Excellency was pleased better with the last and at once put himself in telegraphic communications with St. Petersburg on the subject, and [also] he told me to assure the King that His Crown should not be disturbed as an agreement will be reached on the basis of my suggestion or proposals. If this is done we may be able to make some headway in the many reforms of abuses of long standing and which have so nearly crushed out all spirit for accumulation and industry among the Corean masses which are so much needed.

In addition to this, we have exchanged the ratification of the treaty concluded with Italy. Have just concluded an important treaty—special—with Russia for overland trade between the two countries, and I shall soon take up the subject of extradition treaties, which we want. . . . I hope to be able to take up the various subjects mentioned in your several despatches, and when once up, hope to respond promptly. When the President [of the Foreign Office] handed me your last letter, I asked him to send me all of your unanswered despatches. I would go completely through them; and a few minutes ago he sent them to my office. I told the President that you were an honest and good man, thoroughly in sympathy with Corean advancement, and only too glad to aid her in any way in *your* power or that of your friends.

I need not tell you how pleased we are to have Admiral & Miss Shufeldt with us in Corea as our guests, for this you know already as we are old and tried friends of long standing. I note what you say in yours of the 3rd & 13th of Aug. Have not heard from Mr. Lindsley[38] since coming here, that is, directly. Have had many letters from our good and true friends the Wetmores. We have urged a visit from them & hope to get it in the spring. We have never been more comfortably located in our lives than we are now. No efforts or expenses, I might say, have been spared. You must continue to draw on your stock of patience a little longer, as things move very slowly here. . . .

We have treaties now with China, Japan, U.S., England, Russia, Germany, Italy & France, besides two or three more yet to conclude. It was entirely to my management that the French treaty was made. At one time the feeling was very high between the French minister & the Foreign Office, but I smoothed that down and it was signed. In fact, diplomatic negociations were for a time broken or suspended.[39]

Mrs. Denny joins me in kind regards to you. Please present my best compliments to Mrs. Frazar, whome I have never had the pleasure of meeting but await it with anticipation.

Sincerely yours,
O. N. Denny

His Corean Majesty's Home Office
Seoul, January 4th, 1887

To the
  Directors of the Nippon Yusen Kaisha
    Steam Ship Company
    Tokio, Japan

Gentlemen:

I am pleased to acknowledge the receipt of your reply to my communication relating to the sale of the Steamer "Shima Maru," which I have had carefully translated and laid before His Majesty. It is perfectly satisfactory to me, as I anticipated it would be, and while I have not as yet received a reply from the Palace, I have no doubt that it is to the King.

Very Respectfully,
O. N. Denny
Vice President of the Home Office

LETTER 22

Seoul, Oct. 26th, 1887

Dear Mr. Lo Fungh Lo,[40]

I have not written the second memoranda [sic] for presentation through Mr. Detring to His Excellency the Viceroy, as he seems so bound up in Mr. Yuan that nothing will move him.[41] In addition to Mr. Yuan's official conduct to the King, already carefully laid before His Excellency, he is very seriously compromised officially by the recent scandalous smuggling case at Chemulpo, and which will be fully reported by the Chief Commissioner.[42] If it is the purpose of the Peking Government to keep the present commissioner [Yuan Shih-k'ai] here, it is my intention to leave Corea. When I go I shall be compelled to tell [?] the Chung Tang fully as to the cause of my going. Please give my compliments to His Excellency, and accept for yours my best wishes.

Sincerely yours,
O. N. Denny

Seoul, Corea
Feb. 6th, 1888

Hon. John H. Mitchell[43]
 U.S. Senator
  Washington City, D.C.

My dear Senator:
      The excitement and worry of the last eight or ten months over the conspiracies and intrigues in Seoul and the political complications growing out of China's unjust and high-handed treatment of Corea, and her apparent determination if unopposed by other powers to furnish another example of the "lion and the lamb lying down together" with the lamb inside, has been too much for me and I find my health giving way in consequence. So under the advice of my physician, who advised a change and "absolute" rest, I notified His Majesty that I must leave Corea as soon as a suitable person could be found to take my place, as I should not leave him at this critical moment without some one to advise with in whome the King had confidence. His Majesty would not listen to the change until he had the reports of the two doctors and then had the promise of Mr. Dinsmore, the U.S. Minister here, to relieve me. Mr. Dinsmore is informing his government of the proposed change by this mail, and requesting a reply by cablegram. . . .[44]
The most important thing for him [Dinsmore] in this position, and about the only request he can expect the Hon. Secretary of State to grant, is the appointment of a successor as U.S. minister who is his tried friend, or at least one who will cooperate with him in his honest endeavors to serve the King and his government. I have tasted the bitterness of the lack of such cooperation, for until Dinsmore came I had the opposition of the Legation in all that I undertook to do, with the exception of Capt. Parker, who was not able to do me any good.[45] Col. Long will not be a good successor, for the reason that he is against the Coreans and their country.[46] He sympathizes with no one except Long, whome he regards as the greatest living man, and Genl. McClellan the most brilliant and successful dead man, while such men as Genls. Grant, Gordon, and Stanley were the sons of favoritism and fortune. Can't the

Secty. [Bayard] send Long to Egypt, where he is anxious to go? Having been in the military service of that country, he may do them some good.[47]

When I leave Corea I shall turn the Corean tiger loose on the Chinese policy in the peninsula. I shall not only prick the vassalage bubble, but expose the criminal conduct as well as injustice she has been guilty of towards this little kingdom. If the U.S., Japan & Russia will join in a friendly protest, China will stop. To this end, I shall visit Tokio and St. Petersburg on my way home at the request of the King. I hope to leave Corea by the 1st of April, and will if the government answers Dinsmore promptly. In Japan, I shall publish my brief,[48] then if I go to Russia for the King it will be autumn before I get home. Otherwise I shall be much sooner back. This part of my letter, for the present, is quite private. . . .

Had the Viceroy Li kept his assurances to me in regard to Corean affairs, I might only have gone away on leave, returning in case of improved health. But as it is, I do not care to return even if my health is again all right. The ins and outs of my trouble I must leave until I see you, which I trust will be in a few months. In the event of the government giving Dinsmore permission, which I feel sure they will do as it will make room for another door mat,[49] then write me in Yokohama in answer to this. Do not allow the Chinese Minister to interfere *against* Dinsmore, which no doubt he will try to do under instructions from the Peking government, as they are up to such things. I hope you are in good health [and] are just as active in the interests of your constituency as ever. Mrs. Denny as usual joins me in kindest regards to you and your family, whose health I seriously hope is good.

As ever your sincere friend,
O. N. Denny

LETTER 24

Seoul, March 22nd, 1888

Dear Mr. Wetmore,

Your favors of 23rd and 24th Feb., and 9th [?] of March, came by last mail—very sorry indeed to hear of your illness. Hope you are entirely restored by this time. Enclosed please find a check for $92.22, amount you so kindly paid for me. Should it be necessary I shall telegraph as you suggested. I will do all in my power to get the concessions for Frazar & Co. Before I leave. I want very much to meet you & Mrs. Wetmore in Japan, as I have much I would like to confer with you about; shall let you know when I leave Seoul. No word or telegram has yet been received from the Secty. of State [Bayard] about Dinsmore's resignation to take my place, but he is looking for it daily. If I can carry out the program I am now working on, the political affairs in Corea inside of one year will be quite settled. I think then it will be safe as well as profitable to engage in certain enterprizes here, not for you perhaps, but younger men of your firm. Certainly I would not advise *you* at this day to take any chances in a new and untried field, but stick to Shanghai as long as you remain in the East.

Your criticism of the Peking business is quite just. It seems to be the policy of the [U.S.] government to send men to the East, not to accomplish results, but who will trouble the [State] Dept. the least with violations of treaties and the rights of American citizens. And as you say, the toadying and fawning over the Chinese for *great* favors and small is permitting the Chinese to trample underfoot many of the commercial rights and interests of foreigners guaranteed by treaty stipulations.[50] Every favor granted by the Chinese at the request of a minister which is of a personal nature simply cools the ardor of that minister, more or less, when the rights of his nationals are in dispute. I am at a loss to see any difference in accepting a good position for life—with lots of salary—for a member of one's family while in such a high post as minister, and a fee in money for a given service, although not in the line of one's official duties.[51]

Yes, if I reach home in time I shall take a post in the campaign, not, however, with the idea of returning to the East in the service of the government, but because my heart is in the cause of the Republican party.[52] In the event of success it would not be candid in me to say I would under no circumstances accept a good position if one were tendered. I thank you very much for the confidence you expressed in me in your letter. Mrs. Denny joins me in kindest regards for Mrs. Wetmore and yourself. We hope to reach Nagasaki in April.

Sincerely yours,
O. N. Denny

Seoul, May 13, 1888

Hon. John H. Mitchell,
   United States Senator,
      Washington, D.C.

My dear Senator:
   I have just received a letter from a friend of mine in Peking who is in a position to know whereof he speaks, alluding in pretty strong terms to Minister Denby's unjust and unwarrantable meddling with Corean affairs. If the ponderous Colonel were to pay more attention to the neglected treaty rights of his nationals within his own jurisdiction instead of wasting his time in attempting to prostitute the powers of his high office in tightening the coils of the Celestial anaconda around poor little struggling Corea, his conduct would be more in accord with the objects of his mission, as well as official respectability. My informant says that Denby has written the Hon. Secretary of State[53] assailing the American community in Seoul because they dare to stand up for the independent rights of the King and his kingdom, closing with a bit of advice to the Secretary, that "as the Corean Minister has been duly received by our Government would it not be better to let China have her own way in Corea, rather than to incur her displeasure by opposing her policy here?" What reply the Hon. Secretary made to Denby's impertinence, I of course do not know; but it is fair to assume that he was instructed to attend to his own business and let the U.S. Minister in Corea attend to Corean affairs in so far as they relate to the interests of the people and government of the United States. The Hon. Secretary doesn't know, in all probability, that Denby has violated two provisions of the Revised Statutes since he came to Peking; but such is the fact: One provision is the one inhibiting any United States official from recommending any person for appointment to office in the government to which he is accredited. The other provision is that no official shall receive any present, reward or favour from the government to which he is accredited. I cannot quote the provisions as I have not the Statutes at hand, but I have given you the purport of the Statute on the subject. Now Denby has recommended for and procured the appointment of his

son to a splendid life position in the Royal Chinese Customs Service. In doing this he violated the first-named provision, and in accepting the post for his son or permitting him to accept it, he violated the second. He cannot say truthfully, in extenuation that the appointment was not due to his request and the influence of his position. Other distinguished men, not Ministers, however, have tried to get appointments for their sons in the Customs and failed, for the reason that the rule of selecting Customs employe[e]s forbids it, *except where a quid pro quo* varies this rule; especially is this so now because the staff has a surplus of help. Denby's letter to the Hon. Secretary I hope was not the first service to the Chinese Government because of this request and favour to him in the appointment of his son, and yet it looks very much like it. I should not have written this to you but for the fact that he has been so offensive and indecent in his official deportment. Secretary Bayard, I am sure would reprimand him severely if he knew about his son's appointment, so please tell the Secretary privately what I say, and that you will expose him if he does not attend to his own business, which seems to be principally in looking out for the members of his family. I think if the case were pressed Denby would have to get out;—anyhow, a great scandal would be the result. I, for one, do not propose to submit to his meddlesomeness in this quarter. It seems that nearly every man high and low, has filed his caveat to pounce upon this little country, but their contract will be too broad before they get through with the job. The Chinese are very uneasy; they do not know just where they will get hit next, but they are looking for a dose from me. A good thing comes from "Old Mother" Hubbard, U.S. Minister in Tokio, Japan.[54] He told Major Dee in speaking of affairs in Corea that "you know Mr. Denby and myself exercise a kind of *serenity* or *susanship* over Corea."

My health although much better than it was, is still not what I would like, but the King says he cannot let me go just now on leave of absence even. "You know," says His Majesty "so well what to do." It is quite true I have got him out of some tight corners,—if I do say it myself. Well, you are now about entering upon one of the most desperate political contests our country has ever witnessed, with, I am sorry to say, the odds against us. I wish with all my heart

I were at home to throw in my might or mite, but as I am not, I can only be with you in spirit and in prayer for complete victory.

Write me fully on the situation from time to time. Mrs. Denny joins me in friendly assurances.

As ever your sincere friend,
O. N. Denny

Owen N. Denny (1838–1900) and his wife, Gertrude Hall Denny (1837–1933). (Buchtel & Stolte photo, negative #3447, courtesy of the Oregon Historical Society)

Owen N. Denny, Vice-President of the Korean Home Office and Director of Foreign Affairs, 1886–1890. (A. B. McAlpin photo, negative #53610, courtesy of the Oregon Historical Society)

Kojong, King of Korea (reigned 1863–1907).

King Kojong, seated, and his son, the future Emperor Sunjong (reigned 1907–1910).

Yi Ha-ŭng (1820–1898), the Taewŏn'gun and father of King Kojong.

The garden of Gertrude and Owen Denny, behind their home. Owen Denny is on the far right; Mrs. Denny is third from the right.

Dining room of the Denny residence. Note the combination of Western and Asian furnishings.

Owen and Gertrude Denny, with friends, in their compound.

Mrs. Denny departing in a sedan chair.

Owen Denny, seated, with friends on a winter day in Korea.

Looking northward across Seoul. The Denny residence is on the far left.

Kwanghwamun, late 1880s. Owen Denny possibly is standing on the far right, before the statue.

The Korean port of Inch'ŏn (Chemulp'o), late 1880s.

Group of Westerners in Korea, late 1880s. Gertrude Denny is seated in the middle of the photograph; Owen Denny is near the far right.

Westerners on a footbridge, late 1880s.

East meets West. Note the architecture of the building in the background. The sign over the door on the left reads "Marion's Bar Room."

Korean soldiers, late 1880s.

Part III.

The Controversy over
China and Korea

Seoul, July 13th, 1888

Dear Dr. Eldridge,

Herewith I hand you for your perusal, and therefore for another purpose, a brief I have prepared, setting forth the international reasons why Corea is entitled to independent statehood, as well as exposing the violent treatment she has received for a long time from her powerful neighbor across the Gulf. This paper was prepared in my official capacity, and hence presents authoritatively Corea's side of the controversy and will contribute at least something towards putting the political and other affairs of this little kingdom upon a different basis, unless brute force is permitted to set aside well established rules of international intercourse. In my humble judgment it brushes aside the cobwebs which have been stealthily woven about the Corean problem for the purpose of confounding Coreans and foreigners alike. I have sent a copy of this paper to a Senatorial friend of mine [John H. Mitchell] with a request that he bring up the question in the U.S. Senate, and as the Senator has written me that he should do so at any early date, I apprehend that by this time it has been done.[55]

I would like now to have it published by some responsible paper in Japan in both English and Japanese or Chinese for circulation among the Coreans here. As Captain Brinkley is on the sound side of Corean politics, and as he is one of the ablest if not the ablest writer in the East, I should be glad to have the *Mail* publish and support my paper. Will you therefore, as I have not the pleasure of a personal acquaintance with the Captain, please present my compliments to him and submit the document, and, if he can conscientiously support it, ask him to publish it in both the English and native issues of the *Mail*, sending me a role of each. I sent a copy to Tientsin to a friend of mine, not particularly for publication, but which the Editor of the *Times* has certainly seen, as the Captain will conclude from a perusal of the leader of that paper of June 30th on Corea.[56] Please add my name to the list of subscribers for the *Mail*.

Sincerely yours,
O. N. Denny

LETTER 27

Seoul, July 21st, 1888

Dear Detring,

Your welcome favor of the 12th instant came . . . which I read with much interest. Of course I did not expect you to approve the brief in its entirety, but I had hoped and still hope that the arguments presented in support of the propositions advanced are sufficiently clear and forcible to command respect as the sincere summations of a warm friend of yours; and I assume they do, as the difference between us on this important but vexatious international question appears to be so small. For when you admit that Corea is *not* the vassal of China, but only her tributary, we stand legally as well as practically on common ground.[57]

Touching the appointment of ministers you say, "I am aware that you are not a partisan of Corea's sending ministers abroad in order to establish in the eyes of the world her independence of China." Neither was I in favor of it for that reason alone. In fact in my first interview with the King after coming to Corea, His Majesty asked me about the advisability of dispatching ministers abroad. I replied that it did not seem advisable to do so then—not because Corea has not the right to appoint and dispatch them, but on the ground of expediency, as it would not only provoke opposition but be attended with more or less expense which could be better utilized in the development of the natural resources of the country. The next time I was asked about the matter was after the Minister to Japan had been appointed,[58] which took place while I was up country and without any reference to me. After this, however, having witnessed a year and a half of Yuan's criminal and brutal treatment of the King and government, as well as his interference in the most trivial things, and witnessing the [manner] with which he was supported by his government, I advised—as the only practical way that presented itself in order to cause China if possible to change her course before it became too late—the appointment of ministers to Europe and America. And if that act has the desired effect, it will be the best possible service I could render both countries. At all events the question is now fairly launched and one might just as well try to stop an avalanche as to undertake to smother it before the status of Corea with reference to China is settled. And unless I mistake the drift of international views, other sovereign powers having vested interests here will settle for China what she has lacked either the disposition or ability to settle for herself.[59]

In regard to the appointment of ministers I may add, in addition to what I have already said, that as Corea in the exercise of her undisputed right of negociation concluded treaties with other independent powers with the knowledge and approval of China containing, among other provisions, those for the exchange of public ministers, provisions which have been acted upon by every nation in treaty relations with Corea—except one—the question of Corea's *right* in the [matter], it seems to me, is *res adjudicated*. In any case, now to yield to China the power to render negatory those provisions would carry with it the right to set aside any or all of the stipulations of the treaties in case they prove distasteful to her. [This] would convert the whole procedure of treaty making with Corea into one of the grandest diplomatic farces of modern times. China deceives only herself if she thinks she will be permitted to make other powers seem ridiculous in order that she may carry out her ill conceived scheme of domination in this direction.

While, as you have reason to know, I am just as anxious as you or any other faithful and efficient friend of China's to have the old order of things continued between the two countries because I believe that it will be for the best interests of Corea as well as China, yet I am not prepared to agree with you when you say that "only on the lines which you lay down does the future independence of Corea rest secure from either a Russian or a Chinese dependency"; for in my judgment, either contingency is quite out of the range of practical politics. While China has a keen appreciation of the political importance of the peninsula and is determined—and rightly too—that no other nation shall control it, yet Russia's, to say nothing of Japan's, is just as keen and is just as determined, as China is, that no other power shall absorb it. Herein lies the strength and security of Corean independence. However she may be in all other respects, she is strong in this. It will require a standing army to compel on the part of the Corean people compliance with the commands of either the Russian or Chinese governments, and that, too, without any adequate returns political or otherwise. Russia knows this but China apparently has it yet to learn. The former knew it when the cranky von Mollendorff made his farcical attempt to induce Russia to accept the guardianship of this "Crown of Thornes."[60]

For this reason I regard as chimerical the idea that Russia wants to interfere in any way with the sovereignty of Corea. Neither, in my opinion, can she be induced to assume any more responsibility in affairs here than she has already taken upon herself as a friendly treaty power, but the rights secured and the obligations assumed through this channel I am quite sure she is prepared to defend and maintain.

Neither does Russia seem to be alone in her attitude with reference to the independent character of this country, for she will always have the fullest sympathy, if not the active cooperation, of Japan, as well as moral support of other countries. In 1874 Japan voluntarily [sic] surrendered whatever tributary or other claims she held against Corea as an inferior state, which resulted two years later in the conclusion of a treaty of friendship, navigation and commerce upon the basis of equal Corean sovereignty with that of Japan.[61] Since that time the latter has strictly abstained from all interference with either her political or domestic concernes, bending all her energies and good offices in this direction to the acquisition of trade and commercial advantages. Not only is the rapid increase of Japanese trade over that of the Chinese due in a large measure to kind and friendly intercourse, but it is fast turning the former hatred of the Coreans for the Japanese into friendly regard. No wonder Yuan exclaimed that something must be done to prevent the rapid increase of Japanese trade in Corea. It never seems to occur to him though to look for the cause in the direction where he would be sure to discover it, viz., at his own door. Let China change her Representative as well as her policy and I will guarantee that she will at once begin to recover what she has already lost through the course of her selfish and ambitious lout of a minister—to whom, you say, the Viceroy still clings with such apparent fondness. Well, let H.E. [His Excellency, Li Hung-chang] cling; he only hugs a delusion and a snare.

So far as I am concerned he [Li] has deceived me once too often about Corean affairs to do it any more. H.E. will do just what he is *compelled* to do, nothing more, nothing less. While he has deceived me, he cannot truthfully lay the charge to me of having deceived him. In fact I think I have been too frank to suit the wiles of Asiatic diplomacy. As you know, I have done nothing behind the Viceroy's back. I sent the brief to you for your information, feeling assured that you would make H.E. acquainted with its contents. I told him when last in Tientsin that if he did not take Yuan away and quit meddling with the internal affairs of Corea, I would publish a brief on the situation which would be neither creditable to his government nor pleasant to himself to read. And I have kept my word.

It is reported that the Viceroy is sending over an official to investigate Yuan's conduct and to get at the situation generally. This, if true, in my judgment is to be regretted, for no matter how anxious H.E. may be to get at the truth, he cannot do it in that way. The end would be a *whitewash* of the culprit, which would only make the Viceroy and his government more stubborn on the subject of his removal than ever.

In connection with this business I must confess there is one phase of it I am unable to clearly understand; and that is, the moment it became apparent to intelligent observers that Japan and Russia had given up all designs upon Corea, China herself at once got the disease so badly. But whatever the fact is, we must deal with the situation as we find it, and in doing this I shall do all in my power, in cooperation with you, to bring order and intelligence out of confusion and ignorance. And as before remarked, the very first step in that direction is the removal of the man who has caused so much mischief, together with his Secretary, Tong, who is credited with many of Yuan's schemes. Tong is a pupil of von Mollendorff, which is quite enough in itself. Aside from this, he is without scruples or responsibility. However, with two good men appointed in their place, men of character and integrity who will at all times strive to cultivate close relations with the King and officials alike, a strong flood tide will again set in towards China. In this way only can she maintain her supremacy in Corea. . . .

Mrs. Denny joins me in congratulations for Mrs. Detring and yourself over the advent of the little daughter. We had hoped most earnestly for a son instead, as already you had three such lovely daughters. It will, however, be a great source of satisfaction to you both as well as your many friends to know that the fourth is no less lovely. With best compliments to Mrs. Detring, I am, as ever, sincerely yours,

O. N. Denny

LETTER 28

Seoul, Corea
Aug. 8th, 1888

Dear Detring,

Your favor of the 1st instant is at hand, as also the pamphlets, for which accept my sincere thanks. If you could send me two or three copies, accurately translated into Chinese, I will be under a further debt of gratitude to you. I want very much to discuss Corean affairs face to face with you, as many phases of the question I cannot discuss in any other way. And to do this I would make another trip to Chefoo, if you will meet me there, say the next trip of the Japanese steamer. By that time the Viceroy will have ceased frothing at the mouth over my brief and will, I hope, be a little more reasonable and less radical than heretofore. As much as I always enjoy meeting H.E. and as friendly as I feel towards him still, notwithstanding our differences over the Corean business, yet I never expect to see him again. So if *we* meet it must be outside of Tientsin, as I cannot go to your post as badly as I want to see and talk with you. Will you please meet me at Chefoo?

That old thief and scoundrel of a President of the Foreign Office has been appointed a Governor, so he is out of the Foreign Office. I told the King that unless he was put out of the Foreign Office, I should leave Corea. While it is bad enough to appoint the scoundrel to any position, it is far better than to keep him in a position where by the daily prostitution of the Foreign Office seal he is all the time compromising the King.[62]

The Editor of the Times [the *Chinese Times* of Tientsin] is certainly a strange compound. In one issue, he referred to me as "honest and honorable," and yet he attributes to me dishonorable motives and conduct. I have never done anything to offend him that I am aware of, and yet he keeps snapping at the calves of my legs all the while. It is not at all necessary to be personal in his treatment of the Corean situation. I know very well that many things which appear in the *Times* you disapprove of without your even saying so. While its Editor is sometimes irritating, yet he is often amusing as well as entertaining. In one issue he may be grave, able, and logical. In the next he may appear decked in the war-paint and feathers of the "noble red man"; while in the following he may be in the role of a circus acrobat. In the latter character he made his bow to the public through his leader on Corea in the issue of July 21st.[63]

From the throes and contortions of this Editorial I quote the following: "We might go a step further, and say that to attempt to square the intercourse between China and her tributaries with the maxims of European international law is to subvert the foundations of international law."[64] To say that to enforce a law is to subvert it is about the most absurd proposition that can well be advanced, and yet that is what is here claimed. Then, after delivering himself of this parody, he gallops off to that plain upon which all tyrants stand—the plain of necessity—where he places China above and beyond all laws Divine or the range of human reason in her treatment of Corea. I may now be permitted to go a step beyond the Editor and say that one might just as consistently undertake to *square* a circle by inserting a four sided block of wood as to undertake to show that to attempt to *square* the intercourse between China and Corea by the principals [*sic*] of international law—after they have concluded treaties with western countries and with each other, and after having entered the comity of civilized nations under the assurance that in their intercourse with those countries they would be guided and governed by the long established customs and usages followed by those nations in the past—is to *subvert* and destroy the principals [*sic*] of that law. Both propositions are alike consistent and dignified. This is neither for the eye nor ear of the article Editor, but for you, as showing appreciation of his views of the *fundamental* principals [*sic*] of international law.

I had quite enough of worry and battle over Corean politics and other questions up to the end of March last,[65] and wished at that time to leave, but Yuan and the President of the Foreign Office prevented the settlement of my account for salary already due. And when the King made the payment of this account one of the conditions for a renewal of my contract for two years, I did not see any way out but to accept. Had my salary account been paid I should not now be in Corea. Why these two beggars wanted me to be kept here I do not know, for certain it is that I shall never leave until I am paid up.[66] I have served the King to the best of my ability and he shall pay for these services. If you choose to do so, you may give the Viceroy the purport of my letter to you of July 21st. Don't do so, however, if he is so mad at me that nothing but nails and rat tail files will satisfy him as a regular diet.

Mrs. Denny as well as myself were delighted to hear of the continual progress Mrs. Detring is making back to health again, and also that the little one is doing well. She sends her love to Mrs. Detring and joins me in kindest regards to you all.

Sincerely yours,

O. N. Denny

LETTER 29

Seoul, Aug. 20th, 1888

Dear Mr. Wetmore,

Your favors of the 9th and 11th instant concerning the printing of the pamphlet are at hand. In replying, candor compells me to say that I am surprised and pained beyond measure over the information your letters convey—surprised at your consternation, and pained to think that I, in unwittingly accepting your kind but voluntary offer to superintend the printing of the pamphlet, should have been guilty of inflicting upon so good a friend as I hold you to be such great worry and anxiety as you say the thing has already caused you. The matter is purely the business of the Corean government and my own, and in nowise concernes you beyond your friendly regard for me, any more than it concernes the man in the moon. And now to be informed that in your efforts to serve me you have been caused so much trouble and worry will lead me to profoundly regret for the rest of my life your connection with it. With all my heart I approve of your determination to destroy those already printed as well as every vestige of your agency in the miserable business. For not only would you be untrue to yourself as well as to those who are near and dear to you if you knowingly permitted yourself to be drawn into any thing which might injure your good name, disturb your peace of mind, or endanger your rights of person or property, but I should be supremely selfish and false as a friend if I knowingly contributed any thing towards such an end. Will you therefore out of abundant caution please return to me the type copy I sent you. Enclosed I hand you my check for $60 as under no consideration can I permit you to be put to one dollar of expense in printing or otherwise. Your corrected copy I shall keep to show you at some future time when you will doubtless wish to re-correct it.

It seems to me that in your anxiety to save me from the meshes of the law, you have either undertaken to correct the paper out of existence, or you entirely misapprehend the object for which it was written. Let me call your attention to the fact that it was due to the brutal, high handed, personal and criminal conduct of the Chinese officials towards the Coreans that caused me to make the efforts I have to break it up, and in making those efforts, not to have recited the grievances complained of, would have been [like] the play of Hamlet with that unfortunate Prince left out. There may be some points in the paper which might have been more clearly stated, but these are of such a character as not to materially detract from its force.

At this time I shall only refer to one of your numerous criticisms. You say at the bottom of page 22 I am made to say that Grotius &c. &c. never comprehended the principals [sic] of international jurisprudence.[67] How on earth you could fall into such an error I am at a loss to understand, for surely it cannot be from the language used. I have submitted the point to several persons here, including two lawyers, and without an exception they are all against you. If you will read it over again, you will surely see that it is the absurd doctrine which China is contending for which I claim those expounders of international law never comprehended, and hence did not write about. An illustration may serve to place the matter in a clearer light.

A young lawyer whose client was undergoing a preliminary examination for horse stealing before a justice of the peace proposed to read from Blackstone,[68] when the court wisely informed him that it was no use, as the judicial mind was already made up. "Oh," replied the attorney, "I do not propose to do so in order to change the decision of the Court, but simply to show what a fool Blackstone was to write such nonsense." In a similar ironical way, I undertake to show what fools Vattel, Grotius, and Wheaton were not to have written a chapter covering China's absurd contention, and that the reason they did not write it was because they could not *grasp* such a doctrine.[69]

I have had printed and circulated here 50 copies of the pamphlet such as I sent to you, all but the addenda which will perhaps have the desired effect and which I believe will, in the minds of intelligent people, dispose of China's absurd claims to vassalage over Corea. At all events it will free us from the murderous and depraved conduct of the present Chinese Representative.[70]

> Very sincerely yours,
> O. N. Denny

LETTER 30

Seoul, Sept. 22nd, 1888

Dear Detring,

I am in receipt of your favor of the 12th instant, together with the *Times* [the *Chinese Times* of Tientsin] of the 8th containing a translation from a native paper purporting to give a history of the relations between China and Korea upon which the Viceroy proposes to rest his case—for which accept my thanks. In regard to the latter, I must confess that I have never read a more jerky, disconnected, misleading and erroneous thing in all my life—the vital point of which is the greatest error in it. I do not wish to see the Viceroy further humiliated in his ridiculous Corean business, but he seems determined on showing the fleshy end of his back lower down than decency requires.

For His Excellency's information as well as your own, please find enclosed a copy of the "little yellow book," with addenda on page 11 and a foot note on page 13 which may be interesting. Please say to the would be historical critics that I did not write the pamphlet with a view to contributing any thing in that direction. I wrote it as a *legal argument* and to expose one of the vilest and most corrupt diplomatic agents of modern or ancient times. If at the same time I should contribute anything of value to history, it will not for that reason detract from its other merits. If the question of Korea's continued independence rested on ancient history, I would go back to Noah or the flood and show that Korea has not only been in her present location but that she was at either of those periods entirely independent of China. But this is not to settle it. The question will be disposed of in accordance with those rules of international procedure which have guided civilized and Christian nations in their intercourse for so long, *dating from the time Korea made her treaties with those countries,* and so far as my mind is concerned there is not a shadow of a doubt as to the ultimate result. If the Viceroy wants the darned country bad enough, why doesn't he come and take it?[71]

I am now preparing another chapter on the villainous conduct of the Chung Tang's *pet*. It will be as *black as night,* too, and which I propose to publish if he is not soon taken away. The first was only a gentle slap on the Viceroy's cheek, but the second will hit him square between the eyes and [will be] most compromising not only to H.E. but his government too, detailing murderous plots, assassinations and such with copies of papers, names of witnesses, as well as dates and circumstances. It will be literature of the four "R" brand—rich, rare and racy reading. I do not wish to make it harder for the Viceroy than is really necessary, but the scoundrel must *go,* and that soon. The Viceroy in keeping as the Representative of China at this Court a cut-throat and robber seems to have lost all regard for decency. In the event of the publication of the second chapter, I shall immediately thereafter—based upon it—write an appeal to the treaty powers which will surely do the work.[72]

It shows only the Viceroy's ingratitude when he abuses you because I decline to be a party to Yuan's criminal and brutal conduct. Please say as much to H.E. for me. Neither does the Viceroy do himself any credit in trying to *badger* the King into sending me out of Korea. I am an American citizen *amenable to the laws of the U.S.*, and having a contract with this government for a longer service of 18 months, I would just like to see the color of the man's hair, whether he is in China or Korea, who can *make* me leave before the expiration of my contract, or even afterwards, unless I choose to go of my own accord. I know my rights and I think I have both sense and courage enough to defend and maintain them. . . .[73]

I shall feel badly if the Viceroy erroneously blames you for executing his request to invite me to Korea. A thousand times I have regretted it myself, but I am not such an idiot or ingrate as to in any way blame you for the misfortune.

Thank you very cordially for your suggestion about closing up my affairs with the government, for I know it is the advice of a friend. As I wrote you, if Yuan and the ex-President of the Foreign Office had not prevented their payment last spring, I would not now be in Korea. Yes, I shall meet you at Chefoo with pleasure, as soon after you telegraph me, as I conveniently can, informing you by wire when I leave Seoul and *probable* departure from Chemulpo. I will send only one telegram in order not to attract more notice than necessary. . . . With kindest regards from us both to Mrs. Detring and yourself, I am as ever, yours,

Sincerely,

O. N. Denny

LETTER 31

Seoul, Oct. 12th, 1888

Editor, Chinese Times
  Tientsin

Dear Sir:

    Permit me to call your attention to a few of the errors and misleading statements made with reference to myself in the *Times* leader of Sept. 22nd.[74] In the first place, however warmly, as you say, Yuan may have approved of my selection when the subject was first broached, certain it is that, at the time of my arrival in Seoul, and for some time prior thereto—so I was informed by nearly every foreign Representative here—he openly resented my coming, as he claimed to be the King's Advisor himself, and that my services were not needed. Upon one occasion, when he was harping upon the subject in the presence of one of the foreign Representatives, he was reminded in a kind but candid way that I came to advise the King and Government on matters which he is ignorant of, when the astute Yuan replied that he could take advice of him (the Representative), then warm it over, and give it to His Majesty. About the only offer of assistance or co-operation on the part of Yuan that I now remember to have ever received from him, came soon after reaching Seoul, which was to *intercede* with the King to have my official status fixed as legal advisor to the F.O. [Foreign Office]. But, as I had already learned that the President of that Department was the abject slave of Yuan, either through fear or hope of reward, I declined the honor, great as it was, of becoming virtually the advisor to the Chinese Legation. From that time on, his opposition, vilification, and slander, has been on the increase. Notwithstanding this, I continued to hold friendly intercourse with him until I discovered his murderous plot to dethrone and *destroy* the King, when I broke off all communication with him, as every one who loves peace and loathes crime ought to do. Then it was that he reported that the reason I did not like him was because he prevented me from becoming King or Prime Minister, I do not now quite remember which. You are, therefore, in error when you say there was no jealousy on Yuan's part, or that he received me with "open arms." The character of the people he thus receives I am sure you would not associate with.

You are also in error when you say that "long differences of opinion arose which ended in a bitter quarrel." It was only *one* dastardly plot of his that caused the breach, viz., the destruction of the King and his government. Neither is it true that I was "the nominee of China" to serve the Korean King. The Viceroy [Li Hung-chang] informed me, upon my arrival in Tientsin, that the King having requested *him* to procure the services of a competent person to enter His Majesty's service as advisor, he had, on account of his long friendship and his confidence in my knowledge of public affairs, invited me to the post; and before leaving to take up the line of my duties I had, as I supposed, a clear understanding, not "instructions for my guidance," as to the policy to be pursued. I *was* "to uphold the *status quo* of Korea *vis-a-vis* to China," if you please. I *was* "to advise the Corean Government upon all matters that required reference to a Western Counsellor," and to consult with the Chinese Resident the same as with the Japanese, American, Russian and British residents. I *was* "to promote sound progress and avoid aught that would embarrass the feeble finances" of the state. And I *was* to maintain and defend as best I could the sovereign rights of the Korean King and Government, and *especially* was I enjoined by the Viceroy that, as China was responsible for peace and good order in Korea, to be vigilant on the suppression of intrigues, conspiracies, and lawlessness of every character, and in all things when "necessary" I *was* to report to the Viceroy, and *I have kept the faith pledged*. But in doing so I regret that I have been compelled to hold up to the public gaze a lawless character, whose ruling passion is murderous plots, smuggling &c. The Viceroy no doubt sees and recognizes the picture.

It is true that in all of my efforts in the matters enumerated I was to count on the Viceroy's help, who earnestly, as I supposed, desired the welfare of China's tributary. But I counted on a broken reed, for so far as receiving any assistance or encouragement from the Chung Tang is concerned, I might just as well have appealed to the moon. But notwithstanding the Viceroy's utter callousness concerning his promises to me, it is not true that I have "renounced my former friendship for him"; neither is it true that I have "become estranged from Chinese interests." Only loyalty to the King, whose paid servant I am, has made it necessary for me to oppose their blind folly, as shown in their treatment of Korea; nor is it true that I have "done all I could to induce Korea to break away from allegiance to China." On the contrary, since I came here I have advised and still advise Korea to look to China as in the past for friendly advice and assistance, which you must know if you have read the pamphlet under criticism, for at page 5 my convictions are clearly fore-shadowed. I do not, however, claim any especial merit for this course, as it appeared to be my plain duty in trying to serve the best interests of this government. But, notwithstanding my advice to Korea to stand by her ancient moorings, yet through the criminal and brutal conduct of China's Representative, more or less distrust as to China's friendship and good intentions toward the King and his country has crept into and now disturbs the mind of His Majesty. It was to prevent the breach from becoming irreparable between the two governments, as well as to warn innocent people whose lives and property were being jeopardised and trifled with, after exhausting every effort of a private character, *as you have ample reason to believe,* that I issued the pamphlet, and if on account of this act I am to be accused of estrangement from Chinese interests, and of a renunciation of my former friendship for the Viceroy, then I much prefer to stand in the shoes of the accused rather than in those of the accuser.

Perhaps the estrangement and renunciation referred to is assumed for me on account of something the Viceroy has said or done since I sent him the pamphlet. No, Mr. Editor, I bear no ill-will against the Viceroy or his government. As neither are responsible for China's ridiculous attitude towards this unfortunate little country, when the final "round up" takes place on the "Corean question," even you will have no cause to cast aspersions on my motives or conduct, for you shall then see that I am a better friend to both China and the Viceroy than some of those who flit around the Vice-Regal candle ever ready to tickle His Excellency in the line of his desires, in order to invite a smile instead of telling him disagreeable truths at the risk of a frown accompanied perhaps with something more disagreeable. In the history of our friendly intercourse, the Viceroy, I believe, has never accused me of a want of candour, for no matter how unpalatable the truth has been I have always frankly told it to him, and the Korean business is no exception to the rule. In the past, in addition to the many legal and public questions the Viceroy has consulted me upon, I have rendered some important services, which he has acknowledged in a most cordial way, one of which, at least, I was about the only one in a position to render, and which freed him from annoying assaults of enemies in his own camp, so far at least as the particular thing in question was concerned. Those services were given the Viceroy as free as the wind, for I was always glad of an opportunity to assist him in any way I could, not because of his profound friendship for any foreigner, as in my opinion that has never existed, but because I believed him to be and still believe him to be a patriotic statesman, always on the alert to serve his country to the best advantage, and for that reason the official above all others to whom foreigners have to look for the introduction into China of those reforms and appliances which have contributed so much to the advancement of Western civilization. Perhaps, under these circumstances, it is hardly in place for me to refer to them, or to ask what the Viceroy has ever done in return for the kindness rendered him. If so, please set it down on the weak side of human nature, and let me tell you that about the only thing was to invite me to Korea, where my throat has been in jeopardy more than once perhaps, through the perfidious conduct of his *protege*—an invitation I have never regretted having accepted but once, and that is from the time I turned my face towards the East to accept it until the present moment.

I have understood the Viceroy is angry with me on account of my public criticism of his own course as well as Yuan's villainous conduct in Korea. If this should prove to be so, it will only confirm the opinion expressed above, and will show the Viceroy's friendships to be only ropes of sand, to go to pieces whenever selfish and ignoble schemes come against them. Now, Mr. Editor, I have written you thus at length in order to correct some of the many mis[s]tatements already alluded to, and to leave your mind in an easier frame than it seems to be at present. In conclusion I beg also to remind you that, as a "*very* cautious journalist," you are too far from Korea to speak as positively as you do on matters concerning which you are entirely in the dark.

Sincerely yours,
O. N. Denny

LETTER 32

Seoul, February, 1889

Editor
Frank Leslie's Illustrated Newspaper
New York, U.S.A.

Dear Sir:

The pictures presented in your issue of Nov. 24th last, "from far Korea," are quite correct.[75] But in the 1st and 2nd paragraphs of your comments on the situation here there are statements which are not only misleading but which do injustice to others as well as myself. Will you therefore be good enough to permit a reference to them through your columns?

In the first place I was not appointed adviser to the Korean King by Li Hung Chang, China's Prime Minister. In July 1885, I received at my house in Portland, Oregon, a telegram from Li Hung Chang, the distinguished Viceroy, asking me if I would accept the post of Adviser and Inspector General of Korean Customs, the two positions then being consolidated. The offer I at first declined, but subsequently changed to an acceptance, principally because it came through the Viceroy with whome I had for several years maintained most amicable relations. In view of this, before going to Seoul I went directly to Tientsin in order to confer with the Viceroy as to the policy to be pursued in the event of any material disagreements. I did not propose to go to Korea at all. In my first interview the Viceroy informed me that the King had requested him to procure the services of a competent adviser for Foreign Affairs, and that on account of his friendship with me and the confidence he placed in my knowledge of international questions, he had asked me by telegraph to accept the position. Upon an exchange of views in regard to Korean matters, we seemed to be so nearly in accord that I left for Seoul, carrying with me the assurance of the Viceroy that in all my efforts to preserve the autonomy of the Kingdom and to promote peace and better government, I should have his cordial support.

Arriving in Seoul, I soon arranged the details of my contract, by the terms of which the Korean government obligated themselves to pay every dollar of my salary, after which I received my appointment from the King and entered upon the duties assigned me. As the Chinese Representative here was pursuing a criminal and high-handed policy towards this government, I encountered from the first his bitter opposition. Neither did it take long to convince me that unless I could induce the Viceroy to change it, I must either retire from this service of the King or publicly expose the minister's conduct—but before doing either I determined to exhaust every effort of a private character to bring about a change, which I did, and which included two visits to the Viceroy at Tientsin, all to no purpose.

In the meanwhile, as matters here were going rapidly from bad to worse—the life of the King and his government, including those of foreigners and many native people, being in immediate danger—I determined with the approval of the King to prepare a pamphlet for publication, having for its object the double purpose of presenting the international and moral rights of the King and his government, and warning innocent people of the actual danger which all the time threatened them. The pamphlet was accordingly issued, the first copy of which I sent to the Viceroy himself. The second one I forwarded to Senator Mitchell of my State, with an earnest request that the Senator make it as public as possible. It is the same document, too, which you refer to as a "letter, or memorial." You will see from this that there is absolutely no similarity between my case and that of the late British Minister at Washington to which you refer, for the reason that His Lordship never asked so far as I am able to discover that his political correspondence should be made public.[76]

You err also when you say that "the Chinese Premier makes the greater charge that I have treacherously lent my influence to the intrigues of the Russians," for whatever my offending may have been so far as the Viceroy Li is concerned, His Excellency has never charged me with that as he knows it to be unqualifiedly false. Since I entered the King's service I have labored unceasingly to promote the political as well as the domestic welfare of His Majesty's government, and to that end have done all in my power to prevent the present Chinese Representative from destroying those ancient relations of cordiality and close friendship which have existed between China and Korea for centuries, and which in the interests of both countries ought still to continue. Some of the reasons for this policy are indicated in the following language, at page 9 of the pamphlet alluded to, a copy of which I send you and which I hope you may find time to review in order that you may judge as to whether the legal, historical and moral positions therein taken are not fully sustained. "Their geographical positions, under friendly intercourse, make them a source of strength to each other, while the fact that Korea has drawn largely upon China's population, language, religion, laws, education, arts, manners and customs, which have contributed so much to the sum total of Korean civilization, all combine to strengthen the chain of attachment, and cause her to look to China, as in the past, for friendly advice rather than in any other direction; and in my judgment nothing will interrupt this friendship but a continuation of the illegal and high-handed treatment Korea is now receiving at the hands of the Chinese, and their studied and persistent attempts to destroy Korean sovereignty by absorbing the country."

These views were supplemented recently in an interview published in the Daily *News* at Shanghai.[77] Upon being asked what I thought of Russian intrigues in the capital and would they amount to much, I replied that I do not believe in them. I do not for a moment imagine that Russia could be induced to undertake the responsibility of establishing a protectorate over Korea if urged to do so, thereby incurring the enmity of China. Russia is for conciliating China for the purpose of stimulating and encouraging her overland and other trade. Besides, the difficulty of governing a people like the Koreans, with little or no sympathy with western methods, would be enormous and could only be done by the strong arm of the military. Such a move would at once turn the eyes of the Koreans again, with regret and longing, towards China, from which the conduct of her present Representative has just now more or less alienated them. I know that a few years ago a desperate attempt was made to bring about such a consummation, but it did not succeed, happily for both Korea and Russia.[78] *To such a policy I shall always offer my most strenuous objection.* Nor do I think the King could be led into making such a mistake. What is aimed at is to preserve Korean autonomy, the right to manage her own affairs at home and abroad, and to develop the natural resources of the country—in which I have great confidence—and at the same time keep in tact her ancient tributary relations to China, with the vassal dogma eliminated.

From these views, Mr. Editor, you will see that what I have been striving for, and am still striving for, is a permanent arrangement with China upon the above basis, and a speedy return to the old paths of amity and harmony between the two countries, a basis which would be accepted at once by the Peking government were it not for the ulterior designes of some other powers. But notwithstanding such designes, I believe the policy urged by me will yet be accepted as a solution of the "Korean question."

It is also erroneous to say that a treaty was signed last Sept., or at any time, between Russia and Korea whereby the latter country is assured of the former's protection in case of necessity. The only treaty concluded between these two countries, aside from their general treaty, is one for the regulations of overland trade. This treaty, after having been quite openly discussed from time to time for more than two years between the President of the Foreign Office and myself, on the one hand, and Mr. Waeber the Russian Minister, on the other, was signed a few months ago and is entirely free from any political significance whatever. It is just such a treaty as exists between Korea and China and between Russia and China, the advantages of which under the operation of favored nation intercourse exist alike to all nationalities.

In conclusion permit me to add that I have been perfectly amazed at the slanders, misrepresentation and vituperation heaped upon this little country, as well as upon myself, by a portion of the public press simply because it dares to put forth an effort to maintain its position among other sovereign and independent governments. So far as my own efforts in this direction are concerned, they are the result only of a conscientious discharge of my duty to the King of Korea. I have had no part in the formulation of those wise and well settled rules of international jurisprudence applicable to this case, or in shaping or moulding the historical relations which mark the intercourse between the Chinese and Koreans for centuries, or in the criminal and brutal treatment which the latter people have received at the hands of the present Chinese Representative. My only offense appears to be their presentation to the public as clearly and concisely as my knowledge of the subject enables me to do.

Sincerely yours,
O. N. Denny

Part IV.

Economic and Financial
Development for Korea

LETTER 33

Seoul, Korea
Aug. 19th, 1889

Frazar & Co.
  Yokohama
  Japan

Gentlemen:
    I am requested by the Home Office as well as by General Han[79] to order from Japan through your firm the following goods: 18 picks with handles, 18 shovels, 6 seven pound sledge hammers and 3 twelve pound, with a few extra handles for hammers as well as picks, 6 wheel barrows, 6 axes, 10 cans or kegs of best blasting powder with fuse for same. Please forward these goods by first steamer to Chemulpo in the name of the Home Office, and adding General Han, through me. The money covering this order will be remitted after the receipt of the goods and your bill for same.
                                    Sincerely yours,
                                    O. N. Denny

LETTER 34

Seoul, Oct. 7th, 1889

My dear Mr. Lindsley,[80]
    Your last favor containing a package for the Superintendent of the Royal Mint, as well as a memoranda [sic] for an agreement for the engagement of the electrician now in your employ at Yokohama, reached me two or three days ago. The package for the

Superintendent has been delivered, while the memoranda [*sic*] relating to the electrical engineer has been submitted to General Han, who in turn has laid it before His Majesty. But from what the General [Han Kyu-sŏl] said I do not think it will receive favorable action. In the first place, it exceedes the limits given to Mr. Payne.[81] Secondly, there are too many extras. And lastly, the condition that certain services in the line of his knowledge and profession were to form the basis of extra compensation [seems unacceptable]. As the matter has to be sanctioned by the government, and as they move so slow, I have been prevented from answering you by telegram. In fact, by the time their answer is received you will no doubt be in receipt of this letter.

I also on the 4th instant received your telegram about the embarrassment of the Legation in Washington, which was at once laid before His Majesty (Min Yong Ik being now in Hong Kong), but what will be done about it I cannot say, as the King seems to be pretty well disgusted with the reckless extravagance of the Legation, their ignorant and stupid blunders in business, and their callous disregard of the common decencies of social and moral conduct.[82]

The ignorant, gross and even criminal action of the man selected by Allen and sent out as a mining engineer has brought discredit and humiliation upon the government. Not only did Allen, who was sent with the Legation to keep them out of trouble and protect the name and interests of the government, select a scoundrel and an ignoramus as a mining expert without taking ordinary business precautions apparently against imposition and fraud (one who has already cost this government about $40,000 without the shadow of a chance of a dollar in return), but he [Allen] stood up and introduced to the official and social society in Washington as the wives of members of the Legation two common Korean prostitutes when he had every reason to know they were such. Over these things the King is deeply humiliated and pained, and you can't wonder at it.[83]

Please write Mr. Frazar on the subject and ask him to see the Secretary of State [James G. Blaine] on behalf of the King.

General Han asked me last evening if I had heard any thing from Frazar & Co., or Mr. Payne, about the loan, railway, mines &c. He thought it about time we heard as to prospects, as the government were not only anxious to originate the loan in the U.S., but to have American capital and skill open the ore fields, build railways and other enterprises. I replied that as it would not be an easy matter to arrange these things, he must be patient. In fact, I said while I know Frazar & Co. are doing all in their power to hasten the business along, yet I was sure more time must be given in which to accomplish results. And at this point, I think additional time will be granted if you can report favorable progress soon. I hear that the French are still desireous of arranging the loan. I have replied to all of your letters received to date.

Sincerely yours,
O. N. Denny

LETTER 35

Seoul, Nov. 8th, 1889

Dear Mr. Lindsley,

Since writing you on the 7th of Oct. anent the proposed engagement by Mr. Brenner as electrician in the Palace [and] the reported financial embarrassment of the Legation at Washington as telegraphed by Mr. Frazar &c &c, I am in receipt of your favors of the 5th and 17th of Oct. with reference to Mr. Brenner's proposition. I have nothing additional to report at this time. I may add that his departure for the U.S. I do not think will cause any serious inconvenience to us. As to the pecuniary troubles of the Legation I did nothing more than send the telegram of Mr. Frazar's to His Majesty after carefully explaining the bearing to General Han which it might have on the business of Mr. Payne to New York.[84]

Immediately upon the receipt of yours of the 5th I called the attention of the petty official, who asked Bjerre to send to you for the oil, to that part which said that the goods so ordered had not been paid for and that you did not know what to make of it, whereupon he produced a receipt signed by Bjerre for the money. The next day he called and told me he was in trouble over this, as he was now quite sure that Bjerre was a bad man and had made off with the money which belong[s] to you. He then asked me what he could do about it. I said pay the bill again. This advice he disputed, saying that as he had paid for the oil once for the government, and to the man who ordered it, he thought the government was absolved from further responsibility in the matter. I informed him of his error: that as the oil was ordered by the King's servant for the sole use and benefit of the Palace, Frazar & Company furnished the goods not to Bjerre, who wrote for them, but to the Korean government and that you must look to the government for payment; and that if the government paid the money to a man who had made off with it instead of sending it to you, that it was their fault and not yours and that they would have to pay a second time. Since then I have not heard from him. But I shall press it upon General Han, as also the $107.25 for the tools &c.

His Majesty sent yesterday to ask me if I had heard any thing from Mr. Frazar about the matters entrusted to Mr. Payne while here. I handed [him] Mr. Frazar's letter [sent] to the Home Office, which conveyed his cordial and greatful [*sic*] thanks to His Majesty for the mark of confidence shown him in his recent appointment.

Very truly yours,
O. N. Denny

LETTER 36

Seoul, Nov. 23rd, 1889

Dear Mr. Lindsley,

Since writing you on the 8th instant wherein I informed you, among other things, that your claim for oil had been paid to Bjerre and that he had apparently made off with the money, I am in receipt of your favors of the 20th Oct., Nov. 1st, and telegram of the 18th in regard to sending samples of Ping An [P'yŏngan] coal &c, the contracts of which have been placed before His Majesty through General Han.

Electrical Engineer. The second proposition of Mr. Brenner's I think is being considered favorably. Since the departure of Bjerre, the Koreans have been running the light [the electric plant] without other assistance, but under their inexperienced management I fear the plant will soon become useless, fears which I think

His Majesty also shares, as Han asked me if Brenner could not come sooner than February in the event of his engagement.

Mint Machinery. Prior to the arrival of Mr. Frazar's second estimate, in view of its expensiveness, His Majesty decided not to purchase for the present. Whether the second estimate will cause a reconsideration of the matter, I do not at present know.

The Payne Negociations. His Majesty is expressly anxious about these, especially the loan, as there are some claims against the government which are being pressed and which will have to be met in some way. It has been intimated to me that the Hong Kong & Shanghai Bank at Shanghai is desireous of negociating a loan with the government, but I have pointed out to them that they can do nothing in that or any other direction until we have Mr. Frazar's report, and that as there are other important propositions second only to the loan in value to the government now in his hands, ample time should be given him for that purpose. Mr. Frazar's telegram as set forth in your letter of the 1st instant was very encouraging to His Majesty, as also the one in relation to sending forward Ping An & other Korean coals, as they indicate an active interest on Mr. Frazar's part.

Samples of Ping An & Other Coals. In compliance with Mr. Frazar's request of the 18th instant I have had carefully prepared, lab[e]lled and boxed samples of three kinds of coal which I am sending forward to your care to be sent on to New York by first opportunity. I am placing the box in the care of Mr. John T. Scott, one of the unfortunate miners who came out for the government and who is returning to the U.S. by this mail. Will you please see that he has no trouble with the customs over it and also, should there be any expense in the way of freight &c, please see that he is reimbursed.

I have laid Mr. Frazar's request for further time before the government with a strong recommendation that a reasonable extension be given and I think additional time will be allowed, but the limit of it I cannot tell. I hope you will be able from time to time to report favorable progress, as this is [an] important feature in the situation.

With kind regards
I am sincerely yours,
O. N. Denny

Seoul, Nov. 23rd, 1889

Dear Mr. Frazar,

I received by last mail your welcome favor of 11th Oct. and have given consideration to its contents. As I am in correspondence with Mr. Lindsley, who no doubt furnishes you with such extracts as he thinks will be of interest to you, I shall direct attention to the points touched upon in your letter to me.

The official letter to the Home Office was . . . at once sent to the President of that Department, but [I] have heard nothing in reply. The copy of your letter to the Charge & his reply I have not seen. In future, if there is any matter you wish replied to or wish me to know about, please send to me *first,* then to be handed over by me, as they have petty and poor translators in the different department[s] who wish to make it appear that they are very necessary to the Foreign business, and for that reason I seldom see foreign correspondence relating to business outside of that directed to me.

The departure of the steamers in the winter months from Korea & to Korea are so uncertain that I am unable to give you any reliable data thereon. Sim Sun Teak [Sim Sun-t'aek] is President of the Home Office and Min Chon Muck [Min Chong-muk] of the Foreign [Office]. Pierce never made a report all the time he was here that can properly be termed such, and even if he had, his gross ignorance of mining affairs would render them entirely worthless. A more stupendous fraud never played in any role than he.[85]

I have conveyed, as I wrote you, your greatful [*sic*] thanks to His Majesty for your appointment as business Agent of the government and communicated to the King the points of your letter now being replied to as well as your telegrams, the one of Nov. 1st saying that you have succeeded in "interesting some important capitalists in Korean affairs and hoped soon to report favorably," [and] the other one of the 18th asking me to "send samples of Ping An and other Korean coals," which pleased His Majesty as it showed your active interest in the business in hand. As I wrote Mr. Lindsley, the government are particularly anxious about the loan, as there are some debts being pressed for payment in a disagreeable way and which must be met at no distant day in some way. It is been intimated to me that the Hong Kong & Shanghai Bank is prepared to negociate with reference to a loan to this government, but I have replied that at present the government cannot discuss the question, being obligated in another quarter.

We have only as security for the repayment of the loan the revenues of the Royal Customs, which will amount next year to say $300,000 net Mexican or Japanese Dollars. The interest is to be paid annually, [with the principal being repaid] in a given number of years, say ten or twelve, or whatever time may be agreed upon for repayment. These revenues are not now pledged, except for a small amount which would have to be paid off out of such loan as may be negociated. It must be born in mind that this revenue, though comparatively small now, [is] increasing each year and will continue to do so as time goes on. As you requested in your telegram of the 18th instant, I am sending to Mr. Lindsley by this mail a small box containing samples of three varieties of Korean coal to be forward[ed] to you and which I hope will reach you safely.

No I am not at all surprised at Allen's withdrawal from the Legation and the service of the Korean government after the miserable mess he has made in his efforts at diplomacy & business. He goes to Fusan [Pusan] as a missionary, a calling he is also entirely unfit for. As for being appointed U.S. Minister here, he never had any more show than the man in the moon, as no one knows better than the President and the Secretary [of State] of the importance of having such position in these extraterritorial countries filled by lawyers since they have to pass on the rights of person & property of their citizens.[86] Think of Dr. Allen conducting a trial for murder or an intricate suit at law. It is absurd. This change will not effect you in the least. The King sent to ask me about Brown. As to whether he will stay long, I do not know. His long experience in the State Dept. makes him, it seems to me, a fit man for the post.[87]

Very sincerely yours,
O. N. Denny

Seoul, Dec. 8th, 1889

Dear Mr. Lindsley,

Since writing you on the 23rd of Nov., I have received your favors of the 12th and 18th Nov., respectively, together with a cover from Mr. Frazar with one enclosed from Mr. Payne.

The Mint. The first estimate was so elaborate and expensive that I think it caused His Majesty to drop the matter for the present although they are looking over your second estimate which upon receipt I handed over to the new Superintendent.

As I wrote you, the oil funds were paid to Bjerre, whom the Koreans say has made off with the money. Mr. Pierce is in error when he says the government were in arrears of salary to Bjerre, as his claim was a fictitious one devoid entirely of merit.

I have applied for additional time for Mr. Frazar's negociations which I feel quite sure will be granted, but on account of much excitement in the Palace for the last two or three weeks over the unearthing of another plot directed against the reign and life of the King by the villainous Yuan, business of every other character has been quite suspended. If the Almighty, by a well directed thunder bolt, would make a vacancy in the [residence] of the Chinese Legation, it would surely be good for both man and beast. Just how much this will retard matters here is hard to say at present.

As I wrote you, I sent forward by last mail the samples of coal asked for by Mr. Frazar. Mr. Frazar also asked for a copy of Pierce's report on the Ping An coal deposits, but this is such an idiotic paper that it would do more harm than good I fear. So I have not sent it.

Sincerely yours,
O. N. Denny

LETTER 39

Seoul, Dec. 23rd, 1889

My dear Mr. Frazar,

I am in possession of your favor of Nov. 2nd reporting progress on and asking for certain information concerning the business in hand. I am also in receipt by last mail of a letter from Mr. Lindsley dated Dec. 5th wherein he says, "I have just received the following telegram from Mr. Frazar: 'I have received cooperation of several important capitalists and will advise progress by mail. We expect to be able to contract. Extend time.' "

The contents of both letters I have laid before His Majesty through General Han Kiu Sul. From the above information the prospects for ultimate success certainly look encouraging, although you will yet have many obstacles to meet and overcome before the ends aimed at are achieved, principally arising out of the fact that very little is yet known of the resources and natural worth of Korea, and what is known and said concerning them is from the most unfavorable point of view owing to the most persistent and unscrupulous efforts of the Chinese and their missions to stifle development and progress here by intrigue and falsehood in order to further, as they think, their political designes upon this country.

For instance to show you how flimsey some of their conduct is, sometime ago Merrill, the chief commissioner of Korean Customs,[88] promulgated certain regulations for the conduct of trade between the ports of Mapo, on the Han River three miles from Seoul, and Chemulpo. The Chinese Taotai at Tientsin immediately caused these regulations to be republished over his signature as having been made by himself when it was none of his business, as he had nothing more to do with it than you had. Not only so, but the ignorance of the Taotai caused him to get all mixed up, as he says the regulations are to govern trade between Chemulpo and Jenchuan [Inch'ŏn], the *treaty* name for Chemulpo. Hence, *his* regulations are to govern trade between Chemulpo and Chemulpo, while those regulations which the commissioner issued are for trade between Mapo, near Seoul, and Chemulpo. I refer to this matter here as Mr. Lindsley has written me about it, apparently with some concern. But notwithstanding that law, justice, morality and decency have been violated by China in her treatment of Korea, yet the cause of the latter being just and the country possessing a very high standard of agricultural, mineral & other wealth, she is bound to forge ahead when the political cobwebs which have been so designedly woven around her are brushed entirely aside, which will be the case at no distant day.

The Company. As to its organization, I do not know as I have any suggestion to make [?] or in regard to the name it is to do business under. The promoters will no doubt settle such points all right.

The Extension of Time is not going to be so easily managed as I was given at one time to understand it would be, owing to the fact which I wrote you that the government is now being pressed for the payment of certain debts, the largest of which has been due for a long time to the China Merchants Steamship Co., while the next largest is due to the Japanese as indemnity, together with a number of smaller ones, aggregating in all about $1,500,000 Mexicans. Of course it is desirable to get these claims consolidated and drawing a less rate of interest at an early date; besides, some of these claimants or rather creditors are annoying in their demands for their money. Perhaps the reluctance in extending the time, to some extent, arises from a proposition from one of the Banks in China to loan the government some money, although the sum is not more than half the amount actually needed. However, I am doing all I can for extension, but if granted, I hardly think it will be for longer than three months.

The Loan. Two thirds of [the loan], as I have already indicated, is to be applied to the payment of debts, while the balance, or at least a portion of it, as I am given to understand, [will be used] to establish a bank in Seoul. As I wrote you, the security for repayment of the loan and interest is the pledge of the Royal Customs revenues, which are estimated for the next year at about $300,000 and which are unincumbered, as I am assured and believe, unless it is for $30,000 due to the Japanese National Bank, but which will soon be paid off. The government desire twelve years in which to repay all of the principal & interest so that the amount to be paid on the loan each year can be so graded as to repay the whole within the time specified, bearing in mind the revenues annually available for that purpose.

Coal Samples asked for are now well on their way to New York, the analization of which will enable you to judge of their practical value. At Ping An there do not seem to be, on the surface, any obstacles in the way of easy and profitable mining. Below the surface, however, must be left to boring machinery under the direction of experts in coal mining. Enclosed I hand you an amateur map of the river (Ta Tong) [Taedong] from its mouth to a point where the coal vein crosses the same above Ping An, showing its contiguity to the river, obstructions to navigation, location (proposed) of the port, distances &c.[89] The water abreast of the coal bed, say two & half miles below the city of Ping An [P'yŏngyang], is fifteen or sixteen feet deep; but about fifteen miles below this point there is a shallow reach of about three miles with what is called shingle bottom, where the water is only three & half to four feet at low tide and ten & half to eleven feet at high water. Hence none but light draught vessels can reach a point opposite to the mine, even at high water. For this reason it is proposed to locate the port at the point indicated at the mouth of An Ju River only ten or twelve miles from the Gulf, at or below which the principal coaling station would have to be located in order to enable large draught vessels to take full cargoes. The water abreast of Ping An and above to the point where the vein crosses the river is only four to five feet deep at high tide, but as the coal crops out only two or three hundred feet from where the vein crosses the river perhaps the coal can be more cheaply shipped from this point in native flat bottomed boats to the place where sea-going craft can take it—at least this would surely be so in the beginning. Navigation is closed for about ten weeks by ice in the winter months. The cost of landing the coal on the river at deep water will, of course, depend largely on the facilities of the company for mining and handling it. By this mail I am sending you in care of Mr. Lindsley at Yokohama another small sample of coal which has just arrived from the East Coast well up towards the Tumen River, or this side about 100 miles at a place called Nah Juk Tong [Najŏkdong?] near Kieng Soong [Kyŏngsŏng] & only half a mile from shipping point. The natives use it with great success in their furnaces for the evaporation of sea water in the collection of salt. It seems to have considerable flame but little smoke. The sample comes from the surface and is traceable for a long distance. The vein is said to be at least eight feet in width. In fact coal is known to exist in very many localities in Korea.

Railways. At present I am quite sure that the government will not grant any *exclusive* franchises for railways throughout the Kingdom for a given number of years. At a later moment, if you are on the spot, you may be able to do something in that direction. There are two or three lines which may now be constructed and operated with success. The best one of these, however, in my judgment is the one from Seoul to Chemulpo, which will pay from the start (narrow gauge). There are 250,000 people in Seoul, and at least 300,000 in the suburbs and along the Han River in the vicinity of the crossing, making 550,000 from which the road would surely draw a large native passenger traffic when we reflect that railways are most enthusiastically patronized by all Asiatics, and especially so when they can be carried as cheaply as by any other means. In fact every railway in the East is constantly packed with native passengers and there is every reason to believe those in Korea would prove no exception to the rule, especially when it is the cheapest, quickest, and easiest mode of travel. For instance, a Korean [traveling] by pony from Seoul to Chemulpo & return takes at least two days and [the trip] costs $2, while the railway can take him down and back the same day for that sum or less & make it a good investment. Then again the railway would be patronized by nearly all the foreigners arriving by the four or five regular steamers calling at Chemulpo who are now denied a visit to Seoul as the steamers only remain from 24 to 36 hours at Chemulpo, too short for them to make the round trip. There should be three classes: First Class, one way $2, or round trip $3; Second Class, one way one (1) Dollar, or round trip $1.50; Third Class, one way 50 cts, or round trip 75 cts.

Freight from Seoul to Chemulpo overland by bullock or pony costs $5.50 to $6.00, and by river $4.00 per ton, while the railway can make money at $2 per ton or $2.25 at most. Nor is this all. With cheaper and quicker transportation, much of the freight which is now taken overland by the most direct road to Chemulpo, leaving Seoul to the right or left, would come directly here and be shipped by rail, as it would save both time & expense.

The other points in your letter I believe are more matters of detail than otherwise which can be easily adjusted in the event your efforts are successful. This letter will furnish about all the data I am able at this time to give you. The rest will have to be reported upon by the company experts. As munitions of war, guns &c belong entirely to the Military Dept. and as I have nothing to do with that branch of the service, please excuse me in not refering to the matter here. Thanks for the extra copy of your lecture on Korea, which I shall send to His Majesty. I am indebted to Mr. Waeber, Russian Charge deAffairs here, for the enclosed chart.

Mrs. Denny joins me in best compliments to Mrs. Frazar & yourself and [we] bespeak for you both abundant prosperity & happiness for the New Year.

Sincerely yours,
O. N. Denny

LETTER 40

Seoul, Dec. 24th, 1889

Dear Mr. Lindsley,

After reading my letter to Mr. Frazar, herewith enclosed, will you please seal it up & forward to him. Also please send forward by first steamer the small sample of coal I am sending by the Tsuruga Maru to your care for that purpose. I have for the Home Office taken delivery of the mining goods you sent upon my order. I handed Mr. Payne's letters to General Han which related in part at least to the payment of the money for the oil sent to Bjerre for use in the Palace. The General remarked to me that as the business belong[ed] to another department he could only speak about it, which he would do. I think Allen has reason to feel disgusted with himself for the miserable role he played as adviser to the Legation in Washington. The only wonder to me is that he has the cheek to again put foot in any part of Korea. My compliments of the season to Mrs. Lindsley and yourself, in which Mrs. Denny cordially joins me.

I am sincerely yours,
O. N. Denny

LETTER 41

Seoul, Feb. 4th, 1890

Dear Mr. Frazar,

For three weeks in Jan. I was confined to my house with one of the severest colds I ever had in my life, preventing me from transacting business of any kind. In fact the effects of this attack will hardly, I fear, disappear before the warm weather comes, as it has left me a throat trouble which gives me considerable annoyance. This is the reason that at least two of your letters remain unanswered. Your letter of Dec. 20th enclosing one from Mr. Payne of even date reached me on Jan. 13th, only 23 days from New York, the quickest time on record, and about a week later your favors of Dec. 6th reached me. What delayed them I cannot say. And yesterday I received yours of Dec. 31st. Your official despatches No. 4 & 5 to the President of the Home Office dated Dec. 6th & 30th respectively will be placed before him at once.

Mr. Payne wrote that shortly after I received his letter of Dec. 20th he expected to be with us in Seoul, but the one of Dec. 31st says not until the 3rd week of this month; while in yours of same date you inform me that he leaves N.Y. Jan. 10th & Vancouver on the 20th ex "Parthia." I am anxious for Mr. Payne's arrival, 1st, because His Majesty seems anxious, and 2nd, for the business to go through before delays cause some hitch and the matter fails.

I shall refer to the contents of your letters in their order as dated without reference to the time received.

Dec. 6th. After receiving your cable through Mr. Lindsley, I applied for an extension of time and was assured that the business would not fail for this reason provided it is not unnecessarily delayed. So I did not wire "time extended," as I am sure there will be no trouble on this score and that the government will be prepared to take up your proposals as soon as Mr. Payne arrives. In the meantime, should the business fail, we are certain that it will not be due to any lack of efforts and good management on your part.

I quite agree with you in regard to the importance of replacing the "small fry" in charge of the Legation in Washington. . . . I have urged this upon the King with all the force I could command, while His Majesty has just as often assured me that this will be done. But still it hangs fire. The truth is that since Mr. Cleveland went out, the Chinese seem to have become more "cocky," and threaten the King & his ministers more than ever. Whether any of this is due to a desire on the part of the present Administration to conciliate the Chinese government on account of compulsory treatment she has received on the emigration question, I do not know.[90] But no matter what course the American government may pursue on this question, neither Russia nor Japan will ever permit China to *absorb* this country simply to satisfy an impractical freak. I have fully set forth the law governing the continued independence and international rights of this country—to maintain which international intervention will surely follow should China push her claims to suzerainty too far. Once your scheme is fairly launched things will be better, as then the entire delegation of the great State of New York will come to the support of her capital [investments], and which other senators & representatives will assist. This view of the case is one of our strong arguments here.

Just now many malicious slanders are being circulated throughout the U.S. through the public press in the interests of the Chinese & against this little country. Many of these are written for publication by a couple of disreputable fellows who were recently dismissed from the Korean service on account of villainous conduct. Will you please cause the string of lies published in the Boston Globe of Dec. 30th over the signature of "A. Maurice Low" to be denied. He ought to have signed himself, "A *Malicious* Low."[91] Do not let any of these slanders disturb the business in hand. I shall always advise you of any thing serious. Frank G. Carpenter would be a good man to refute these slanders as he has been here and knows the situation. Cannot you get interested *for* Korea? One Shanghai paper is red hot against the Chinese course in this country.

Your Dec. 20th. You may rest assured that I have kept the matter constantly before the King and the officials since Mr. Payne left, while all letters & cables have been translated and discussed as they have from time to time been received. There is no idea of a Russian railway along the East Coast to Lazereff. This will be for your company to consider when you come. I have, though, urged the building of a telegraph line from Seoul to Vladivostock which will give us the cheapest cable & telegraph rates in the world with Europe & the U.S. I regard this as most important & which will be a profitable one too. The line can be cheaply built; shall talk with Mr. Payne about this when he comes. The rate from Vladivostock to Petersburg I believe is about 5 cts a word.

Yours of Dec. 31st. While I agree with you that extension of time is not necessary, yet I asked it out of caution. The reason I am sure the King did not *formally* extend it is because it might delay matters; that is, you might take more time than you otherwise would. You know they do not understand very much yet about western business methods.

The area of Korea is about 85,000 square miles, & population is safely put at 12,000,000. The other questions I have not sufficient data upon to express an opinion. I have asked Mr. Payne to be my guest while here.

Sincerely yours,
O. N. Denny

LETTER 42

Seoul, March 22nd, 1890

My dear Mr. Frazar,

Owing to the callous indifference of the government, in whose service we are, about keeping the faith of their obligations either expressed or implied I have not had the heart to write anent the business of last August since the arrival of Mr. Payne at my house one month ago until now, and while the miserable turn affairs have taken will be exasperating and disappointing to you and your honorable associates, yet it may console you just a little to know that it is what I have had to put up with ever since I entered the King's service more than four years ago. And yet while this has been my experience as an employee of this government, I thought and believed that as the King had requested me so urgently and often to try and carry through some such scheme, if undertaken it would be concluded on the lines usually governing such transactions, especially so, since you had succeeded in getting from His Majesty authority under the seal of the Home Office to take up and discuss preliminarially [sic] the best terms offered by the bankers for the loan as well as for the internal development of the resources of Korea, and although this authority in the eyes of western businessmen may not amount to much yet others have tried very hard to get such authority and signally failed.

Mr. Payne at once handed me all papers, data, etc. with which he came provided bearing on the business in hand, including copies of your correspondence with . . . the President of the Home Office, two Powers of Attorney for execution here, together with your favor to me of Jan. 10th with its enclosures, also of Jan. 11th. Prior to that I had received your note of Jan. 2nd and subsequently your favors of 16th, 28th, 29th & 30th Jan., and 7th Feb., with their several press copy enclosures of former letters, all of which have had my careful perusal.

On Saturday, Feb. 22nd, I informed His Majesty that Mr. Payne would arrive that evening prepared to lay before the government your proposals, and on the next day I received word that the Presidents of the Home and Foreign Offices would be sent in three or four days to my office to discuss them with Mr. Payne. In the meantime I went carefully over the points submitted, noting the conditions liable to be objected to by the government, but before discussing these at length with Mr. Payne, I deemed it my duty to call his attention to those events which had disturbed the quiet of the situation since he was last in Seoul.

1st. The Palace last Dec. was thrown into a great state of excitement for two or three weeks over the discovery of a secret society said to have for its objects the overthrow of the King and the government, several members of which were arrested and punished.

2nd. No sooner had the excitement from this source subsided than the Korean merchants of Seoul on their New Year's day (Jan. 21) closed their shops and refused to open them again unless the Chinese and Japanese merchants were sent out of the city, justly claiming that as they were heavily taxed by their government they were unable to compete in trade with the Chinese and Japanese who paid no taxes at all. For six or seven days their shops were closed and no business done in the city: naturally the tension became very great as many poor people who live from hand to mouth had to go hungry, but finally the merchants were induced to open business under a guarantee from the government that every effort possible would be made to fairly adjust the matter and to this end an official has been sent to discuss it with the Viceroy at Tientsin, Yuan here refusing to do so. What the outcome will be we of course cannot tell, as it involves yielding rights acquired by treaties, which as you know, are always most stubbornly insisted upon. The merchants declare that unless their demands are acceded to, they will again close, let the consequences be what they may.

Another point I called Mr. Payne's attention to is the extravagant and criminal waste of the public funds, and that in the event of your contracting with them, you should insist upon the creation of a Board of Finance or Control composed, say, of three high Korean officials and at least two foreigners and that no contracts for the expenditure of money should be valid unless approved by this Board. Had such a Board been created three years ago when I pressed so hard for it as well as many times since and which has been repeatedly promised by the King, I am certain at least a million and a half of dollars would have been saved for legitimate enterprise, which has been worse than thrown away, having been squandered upon corrupt jobs and which has so seriously crippled the government financially—and that it should also be stipulated that all the floating debt of the government should be paid off out of such loan.

In discussing with Mr. Payne the merits of the propositions submitted by the bankers as well as those of the proposed American Co., I pointed out that in my opinion the following conditions would meet with strong opposition on the part of the government:

1st. With more than half the entire loan retained in the possession of the Company to be by it managed for internal development, and with the interest payments secured in the amount of the loan, the bonds of the government at .78 would be too heavily discounted.

2nd. Deducting two years interest on the amount of the loan from the sum paid over to the government, instead of one.

3rd. The number of years the company should control and operate the Railway & mines and the amount of profits it should receive as services therefor.

The foregoing were some of the principal points which were being discussed when late in the evening of the 28th of Feb. the Presidents called at my office, but as they came without giving any notice, it so happened that Mr. Payne had gone out for a short walk and did not see them on that evening. Upon expressing regret that they did not inform us of their intended visit, in which event Mr. Payne would have been present, they said they came in pursuance of the commands of the King to talk over the business of the loan. They remembered that last August their King through the Home Office had authorized Mr. Frazar, the Korean Consul General in

New York, to try and arrange for a government loan, and now Mr. Payne had returned to their country for that business. . . .

But since that time the government had decided that to build Railways would so excite the people that serious disturbances would follow. And as to the loan, they said, after again asking about the rate of interest, if they took so large a sum of money they could not repay it. Not only so, but as the King needed all the revenues from the Customs from time to time, they could not pay the interest as it became due. For these reasons they wished me to say to Mr. Payne that the government had decided not to negotiate any loan now or in the future. As these were light and even frivolous reasons, knowing that the government desired a loan now just as much as last August, I attached at the moment no significance to them further than a desire on their part to lead Mr. Payne to believe that the government is quite indifferent as to whether they secure a loan or not in order to affect favorably any negociations which might follow. In fact after having expressed so much solicitude about the rate of interest I fully believed they would hear and discuss in good faith your proposals—and as these differed materially from the line of those discussed last August with Mr. Payne, I thought to prepare their minds for this by saying so, at the same time adding that while this was true and while they will have to be amended in some important particulars perhaps, yet I thought this could all be arranged when they came to discuss the proposals at length with Mr. Payne, whereupon they took their leave.

On the 3rd instant I received a letter from the President of the F.O. saying that the government had already talked over the loan business and decided against it, and for me to inform the agent of Frazar Co. "of this." The decision was made without any knowledge on the part of the government as to the nature of the proposals, as they did not know and do not now know the character of them; and as to what the President says I told him about them, it was as I have said above. Surprised at the contents of this letter I thought perhaps we had not understood each other owing to the inexperience of their interpreter and so informed His Majesty.

Thereafter, on the 15th instant the Presidents called again with a different interpreter and in the presence of Mr. Payne they asked me if I had sent word to His Majesty to the effect that perhaps we did not understand each other on the subject of the loan, and I replied that I had. They then repeated substantially what they had said before and asked Mr. Payne if he now understood them, when Mr. Payne replied that he did—that their ears were closed while his mouth was closed—which ended the matter and the Presidents left.

In the meantime rumors were floating in the air of preliminary arrangements having been made with the Japanese for a loan of 2,000,000 silver dollars secured by the Customs revenues, supplemented by concessions to work the coal beds of Ping An and other places for a term of years—or substantially upon the basis of our talk with Mr. Payne last year—the railway scheme from Chemulpo to Seoul being left out so far as I am able to learn at present; rumors which have since been confirmed. Nor is this all, as I am now morally certain from small events happening from time to time, but which did not cause me to anticipate their drift, that the scheme for the Japanese to make a loan to the Koreans began to take form as far back as Sept. of last year through the efforts of General LeGendre, of whom you may know, acting in concert with the Korean chargé d'affaires accredited to Tokio.[92] The activity of the Japanese officials, bankers and merchants, displayed last autumn in surveying the Tatong [Taedong] river, examining for trade capacity of the Province of Ping An, as well as surveying the coal fields, was believed to be in the interest of opening that port [P'yŏngyang] for commercial advantages, but it now appears to have had a broader significance. In the same interest, the Korean chargé d'affaires left Tokio last autumn for Hong Kong to consult Min Yong Ik, and while I was assured by Gen. Han a few days ago that Min did not approve of the scheme, yet I am inclined to believe that he did, as after the return of the chargé to Japan in Dec. the Koreans seemed to manifest less interest in the progress you were making than before, not only so but Min has not written to me since that visit.

When Mr. Payne arrived in Chemulpo he found LeGendre there, who seems to be a prominent figure in this business. LeGendre had been there about ten days consulting with the notorious Allen who introduced the Kisang girls to the society of Washington as wives of members of the Legation.[93] The same day Mr. Payne came up [from] Chemulpo, LeGendre also reached

Seoul, and co-operating with Kim Ka Chin, the Japanese began an active campaign for their scheme aided by Koreans favorable to it. In about a week thereafter Yenami, manager of the branch of the 1st National Bank (Japanese) here, left on important business to Tokyo believed to be in connection with the proposed loan and concessions here—and a few days subsequently LeGendre was gazetted as a Vice President of the Home Office,[94] and it is said, whether truthfully or not I do not know, that he is to be assigned to the head of the Customs in the event there is any obligation on the part of the present commissioner to pledging their revenues for security for the proposed loan.

Of course it is perfectly legitimate and proper for the Japanese to loan the Koreans money and to work their mines and also to get the Koreans to appoint their friend to a position whereby their interests will be properly guarded. But in the execution of the proposed arrangement it seems to me that the Korean government has failed to consider an almost insuperable obstacle, viz.: the Chinese who are already over sensitive in regard to what they claim to be traditional and vested rights in Korea. And as the contest for commercial supremacy in the peninsula is between the Japanese and the Chinese, to say nothing of the political aspirations of each, the latter are sure to resent as impertinent any concession to their rivals which will enable them to in a great measure dominate and control the situation. Under such circumstances I shall be surprised if the Japanese program does not go to the wall, but just what the situation will be when that occurs I cannot tell.[95]

You will easily see from what I have said the cause which brought your negociations so suddenly to a close. Being still the paid servant of the Korean government and [given] the part I have taken in trying to arrange a preliminary basis for the business to proceed upon . . . at the earnest request of His Majesty, I am estopped from indulging in adverse criticism over the result. Not so, however, with you and your associates, as in the history of the case you and they will no doubt find much to complain of and be disappointed over. At the same time I must express my profound regret that after you have expended so much time, labor and expense over this business that it has so far come to naught, and can only hope that the result of these efforts may yet prove in some way beneficial to you.

In ten days more my second contract expires and although having been urged by His Majesty nearly three months ago to renew it, I delayed until recently my answer in the hope that the arrangement contemplated with you might be made, in which event under certain guarantees on the part of His Majesty I should have consented to remain for another term in the hope of seeing the fruits of my faithful and unceasing efforts in behalf of these people ripen. But now it is my fixed purpose to leave Korea as soon as I can arrange to do so.

I have not delivered your letters to the President of the Home Office bearing upon the business in hand for the reason that there is absolutely no security against having the contents of such letters hawked about the streets of Seoul and from there to the newspapers; and as reference was made in them to persons high in official life, I knew my action would meet with your approval. I shall hand them to Mr. Payne to be returned to you for revision or such disposition as you may desire to make of them.

Sincerely yours,
O. N. Denny

LETTER 43

Seoul, April 8th, 1890

My dear Mr. Lindsley,

The situation so far as your business is concerned has not changed since the departure of Mr. Payne. Quite a strong under current, however, seems to have set in against the employment of LeGendre, and which is opposed more or less to any loan from Japanese sources. My own opinion is that the Japanese loan will fail, which will send LeGendre "to the wall," as his employment is only a condition precedent to the negociations by him of the loan. Whether, in the event of his failure, the government will again turn to Frazar & Co., or whether, in such a contingency, they would care to take the chances of being further triffled with, remains to be seen.

So far as I am concerned, I am not only prepared to but desire to give up all further efforts in this quarter upon the settlement of my account and return home, which I can do with a clear conscience, as I have accomplished for the Koreans all that any one could accomplish in the same time, and all that they would *permit* me to accomplish for them. Had my advice been followed, both their political and financial affairs would now be upon a much better footing. This, however, has been prevented by an army of small, corrupt and unpatriotic minds.

With best compliments to Mrs. Lindsley & kind regards to Mr. Payne, I am

Sincerely yours,
O. N. Denny

LETTER 44

Seoul, May 3rd, 1890

Dear Mr. Lindsley,

Your favor of April 17th reached me by last mail. It does not surprise me that you should characterize as shameful Mr. Frazar's treatment by the Korean authorities. As for myself, it is about what I have been subjected to ever since I came to Korea, treatment which would have become unbearable before this last but for the fact that they have treated *all* the representatives of other governments here in a similar way.

But the part of your letter which did surprise me was to learn that LeGendre is not a truthful person, for when he says that "Mr. Frazar's report was carefully considered at conferences at which he was present, and that the Minister of the Home Office called upon me in person and stated that they could not be entertained," he should be denounced as one of the biggest liars in the East. The Presidents of the Home and Foreign Offices called upon me twice together. The first time they said, "we cannot build railroads in Korea as it would excite the people and that the government did not want to borrow any money now or in the future as they needed all the customs revenues for other purposes and so could not pay back the money if they were to borrow it." This they asked me to tell Mr. Payne. I then said, as the propositions are different from those talked over last August, and which would have to be modified in some particulars, to see Mr. Payne and hear from him what Mr. Frazar's proposals are.

The second time they called they reiterated this. Mr. Payne was then present, but they would hear nothing from him on the subject. The papers Mr. Payne handed to me upon his arrival, relating to Mr. Frazar's business, were never out of my possession until I handed them back to that gentleman just before his departure. Neither did I state the proposals to any living soul in Korea, and as the Koreans did not then know, it was impossible for old LeGendre to know what they were. Neither do I think any idea of them was gotten from me. Mr. Frazar's letters to the Home Office, as all those letters addressed to that Department through me, were returned to Mr. Frazar through Mr. Payne for such further disposition as he thought advisable. Of course Mr. Frazar *may* have sent others directly to that department which I did not see, but I doubt it.

Nor is this all. A high Korean official called upon me about a week ago and told me that the government do not know what Mr. Frazar's proposals were; that fully two months before Mr. Payne's arrival the government had decided not to further discuss the matter with Mr. Frazar & that *this was one of the conditions enacted by LeGendre, through Kim Ka Chin*. The old beggar's attitude in this business is a *lovely* one, is it not? Had you only thought to have asked him to tell you what the proposals were at the time he virtually told you that Mr. Frazar's propositions were so dishonorable that no government could accept them, you would have unarmed him completely; in other words, you would have struck him "dumb as an oyster."

There is no doubt but what LeGendre & Morse Townsend & Co.[96] will act together should he be permitted to stay here—which I seriously doubt—as "birds of a feather" &c. LeGendre would not, on account of conduct in China,[97] be [useful] were he to be appointed by the U.S. to any office there. Under such circumstances do you not suppose that they will make it so tropical for the King as long as the old beggar remains in the King's service that His Majesty will curse the day he ever heard of the name LeGendre. He has, I hear, gone to Hong Kong to make his peace with Min Yong Ik, a difficult task I apprehend.

I hope to get my accounts settled so I can get away next month. Mrs. Denny joins me in kindest regards to Mrs. Lindsley and yourself.

Sincerely yours,
O. N. Denny

LETTER 45

Seoul, June 1st, 1890

My dear Mr. Frazar,

I am in receipt of your favors of March 17th and April 18th respectively, the latter containing press copy of the former. Since my last letter to you, old LeGendre's wind-bag has been punctured and he has collapsed—failed in all his great promises to the King, which will no doubt send him out of Korea with his nar[r]ative between his legs, having accomplished nothing in this direction except the further consideration of your proposals, and that too, by the most contemptible means imaginable. The Korean government feel that he has outrageously imposed upon them and it would not surprise me if they would, as they ought to do, apologise to you and invite a consideration of your proposals again.

No doubt Mr. Lindsley has sent you a copy of my letter to him of May 3rd wherein I comment . . . on LeGendre's conduct [and] business. Mr. Lindsley writes me that LeGendre had the monumental impertinence to say to him in his office, after repeated assurances of his friendship for your firm and a desire to co-operate with you in Korea, that not only were your proposals of such a character that no government could entertain them but that he proposed to operate with Morse Townsend & Co. as the Koreans were under obligation to Morse. This I have informed to the authorities here; information which will not tend to add to the strength of LeGendre's cause as the Koreans are not only under no obligation to Mr. Morse, but their experiences with Morse Townsend & Co. are of such a nature as to cause them regret at having had any business relations with them at all, LeGendre to the contrary.

I cannot yet say when I shall be able to get away, as my account for salary has not yet been adjusted. I can't say either that this is a source of regret, as I desire to see LeGendre *kicked* out before my departure as an act of retributive justice.

Sincerely yours,
O. N. Denny

P.S. Mr. Heard is now installed. He seems a clear-headed, reliable man & I think will make a good minister.

LETTER 46

Seoul, June 1st, 1890

Dear Mr. Lindsley,

Your favor of May 3rd came by last mail. The enclosed letter to Mr. Frazar,[98] which I have left unsealed for you to read, is all I have to say at present anent matters here. LeGendre having failed to make good any of his promises to the Koreans, will no doubt make his official connection with the Korean government of short duration.

Mr. Heard, having had to wait for audience, on account of sickness of the royal family, until Monday last, only took over charge on that day. I think he will make a good minister & get on well here.[99] My information is that Min Yong Ik does not approve at all of the LeGendre business and that he so told LeG. at Hong Kong. Neither does Min belong to the Kim Ka Chin clique, whose sun will be of short duration. In fact Kim is now held responsible for having made a fool of the government over the LeGendre fiasco, and when the one goes to the wall the other will.

Sincerely yours,
O. N. Denny

Appendix A
Newspaper Articles Related to
O. N. Denny's Korean Activities

Corea[1]

This unhappy kingdom, which seems likely to be a bone of contention between the three Empires concerned, is again in trouble. Various alarming messages were received some days ago, some actually stating that a rising had commenced and that blood had been shed. Happily, so far, the report has not been justified by fact, although the situation is serious and alarming. The populace were greatly excited against foreigners and threatened to kill them, but by the latest account the people are more pacified, and the ebullition seemed to be subsiding.

There are at least four political parties in the kingdom conspiring for power. There is the King's party, which is in possession, and in this respect, though honeycombed with disaffected officials, has a distinct advantage. On the whole this party aims at independence, while it trusts ultimately to foreign help to effect a complete and final rupture of all ties to China. This faction is really led by the Queen, a bold and clever women, whose mind is swayed by two powerful impulses—the impulses of a strong individuality—personal ambition and patriotism. It is possible she may represent correctly the vague but actual desire of the people, and we should judge by some papers that have appeared in our columns that there is in Corea a distinct national feeling, and that the people recall traditions of their past history when Corea struggled not ingloriously against both China and Japan.

The sentiment of nationality has deep roots, and if the Queen is, as some assume, the leader of the popular spirit, it will be necessary for China to deal with the fact and to shape a new and reversed policy accordingly, so as to bind Corea to the Empire by enduring bonds of amity and common interest, a policy quite practicable if the statesmen of the Empire can rise to the occasion.

The second party is scarcely less powerful than the first; in fact, if serious conclusions were tried [it] might prove to [be] superior, if only on account of better leadership. This party is that of the Dai-in-kun [Taewŏn'gun], and includes the most powerful of the nobles, many ex-officials who are still influential, and a following—no doubt consider-able though it cannot yet be defined—amongst officials and even high Ministers. This group, while it has national aspirations, declares that, for the present at least, it desires rather to put the kingdom into more distinct contact with China than to part from her, and indeed wishes to become assimilated to China in many ways, such as with the army and navy, customs, foreign relations, etc. Naturally Yuen [Yuan Shih-k'ai], the Chinese Resident, has close relations with this faction, and it is said, though the statement seems to be anomalous, that his chief ally, the Corean Prime Minister, is a partisan of the Dai-in-kun. If this is really the fact, the conclusion we draw is that the second party, which means to dethrone the King and to set up instead a child under a Regency, is so strong that the Queen, bold women as she is, hesitates to bring matters to an issue. For the rest the Dai-in-kun is a stern man, not burdened with scruples, who will not shrink from decisive action when the times are ripe for it.

There is a pro-Russian faction, not numerically strong, and, fourthly, there is a pro-Japanese faction of more considerable dimensions. But as regards this last it should be said the Japanese Resident has strict orders from his Government to stand aloof from all political intrigues, and that he obeys his orders loyally. Any influence he may have, if used at all, is on the side of China.

The disturbing elements of the present situation have been growing steadily for several months. The position of the Government has become almost intolerable. The finances of the kingdom are in a bad way. There are old burdens dating from the time of Mr. von Möllendorff's office, for which, however, he may be partly blameless. The social affairs of the country are, seemingly, in the first processes of transition, as no doubt the hereditary privileges of the nobles and official classes will soon have to be abolished. It is quite possible the increasing popular feeling against the abuse of power and immunity may be the real cause of the present commotion. The situation, already troubled, is complicated by the ex-cessive friction with China, or, perhaps, to speak more accurately, with the Chinese Resident, as it cannot be ascertained clearly whether in his unfortunate relations with the King and Court he is following his own scheme of policy, or acting more or less in accordance with definite official instructions.

A very serious additional element of disturbance was the re-appearance a month since of Mr. von Möllendorff upon the scene of his former and well remembered and erratic achievements. It was believed that he went from this place [Tientsin] to Seoul with specific ends in view, amongst which were, it was said, an intention to aid Yuen in his struggle with the

King, or to bring the King to the side of Yuen; also to seize charge again of the Customs, whose control is now vested in the Inspectorate-General at Peking. These imputed aims are apparently antagonistic, so that we do not give full credence to the current rumours, as if, for instance, Mr. von Möllendorff really has any designs on the Customs he could hardly hope for the support or countenance of the Chinese Resident.

Mr. von Möllendorff's advent, misunderstood as its real objective is at present, had the unfortunate result of at once making Japan restive and suspicious, as Mr. von Möllendorff's former policy, which made straight for St. Petersburg rather than towards Peking, was not recalled with complacency at Tokio; and, as is natural in Eastern countries, the Japanese Government, which contrary to many national traditions has for three or more years acted toward China with excessive amiability and forbearance, began to regard his return to Seoul as a signal of bad faith on the part of Peking; and such being the case, especially as Kuroda who was a party to the Japanese treaty with Corea in 1875 [1876] is now in power in Tokio, a few accidental or unfortunate circumstances might quickly raise excitement in Japan, and re-inflame old jealousies, supposed to be laid at rest in such a way as to make continuance of alliance and peace with China uncertain. China should, therefore, now consider the details of Yuen's proceedings, as there are serious reasons for doubting whether they are fully comprehended here. And the more so because China is legally compromised by the acts good or bad, authorized or unauthorized, done by her representative.

In some ways, however, the situation has improved, or rather recent occurrences might by right management be turned by China to good account. Great humiliation has lately been brought upon the King and his Government, which both now feel acutely in a painful awakening. The Corean envoys to foreign courts have been snubbed; their endeavours to raise loans have been foiled, and not even have they anywhere been able to evoke sympathy. The King is thus thrown back upon China, or, as an alternative—if China does not reverse her present policy and methods of action in Seoul—to his vain quest for independence. At any rate the King is now in many respects free from illusions, and while he is smarting from the consciousness of failure the time is opportune to bring him by gentle means again into harmony with China. The Court of Peking certainly has benevolent intentions towards its vassal, and if good conduct in the future was assured the credit of China might be used to raise the impoverished kingdom out of its difficulties. A little show of amity, a few proffers of help, some assurances that all past doubtful behaviour is condoned, and Corea may again come of her own will into the Chinese fold.

Peking now sees the situation has become full of danger not to Corea only but to the Chinese Empire, and may yet we trust change the present dangerous procedure, while it is possible to do so. If the imperious needs of the preservation of the Empire should force the statesmen of Peking to take armed action, they will be justified when called upon to answer for their conduct. But if China is compelled to absorb Corea, the other nations concerned will require good and sufficient reasons from her to justify her course. For armed intervention and occupation China must have clean hands to show, and will have to produce an adequate pretext. If it should be necessary to depose the King—and Yuen is in alliance with the Dai-in-kun's party which aims at this step—the course must have weighty justifications. It is not a slight matter, and unless he can prove urgency or necessity Yuen will find his course is dangerous to himself. The responsibilities of the situation any way lie upon China.

As the unhappy King knows that Yuen is planning his deposition, how can good feeling exist between the two governments? Besides the King complains, how truly we know not, that he is subjected to constant contradiction, obstruction, and affront, and that he does not receive from the Chinese Resident the conventional respect that is due to a monarch. The King's position indeed has become pitiable. Now the policy of China in a country upon whose future status much of the fortunes of this Empire depend, should be to foster amicable relations, to give friendly and loyal assistance when needed, to abstain from party intrigues, to uphold the Throne, to avoid needless meddling, to provide a sympathetic Resident, and in all ways to promote the peace, comfort, and prosperity of her now suffering tributary.

The situation requires very great caution in dealing with it, as quite apart from the interests of the little kingdom, China has grave reasons for rather averting than precipitating a crisis in Seoul; but until sincere and amicable relations are established with the King, his government cannot devote themselves to the reforms he is anxious to make so as to improve the welfare of his people. Yuen, whose conservative ideas are those of a Chinese official who has had no contact with the West, regards change from a too purely Chinese point of view, and, so far, has effectually obstructed all attempts to begin the necessary modifications. This is to be regretted, as in many ways the conditions of Corea are not those of a Chinese province, and the policy of Liu-ming-chuan in Formosa should be held out to him as the right model for imitation. It would be far better to give the King a free hand and to place confidence in his loyalty, and it might be possible for him, if he had to deal with friends rather than with hostile censors, that he might raise the fortunes of his kingdom and at the same time form a strong outwork for protecting China on what is now her most insecure frontier.

The methods in vogue for the last few years between China the suzerain and Corea the tributary, have proved detrimental, and, according to appearances, China may at any moment find herself immersed in difficulties equal in magnitude to those of Annam-Tongking [the 1884–85 Sino-French war over Annam], but with weaker moral bases, and with greater potential difficulties that may develop prematurely. These old methods having ignominiously failed, and as in consequence dangers are arising to involve both Empire and Kingdom, the Viceroy Li will now do well to try a change of front. He might gain—as a result—a loyal, devoted, and firm adherent in the King, who is now deeply alienated from the Empire.

ARTICLE 2

Corea[2]

We commend to the attention of all who are interested in Chinese international policy the very practical and ably written article which we have extracted from the [London] *Times* of 31st May. The writer shows clearly that to discuss the relations of China with her neighbouring States on the basis of European international law is a mere beating of the air; for, although Chinese polity existed before European international law was thought of, the status of the Far Eastern countries was unknown to and ignored by the writers on that variable and uncertain science. We might go a step further, and say that to attempt to square the intercourse between China and her tributaries with the maxims of European international law is to subvert the foundations of international law, which is no authoritative revelation from above, nor the dictum of any power on earth able to endow it with an efficient authority, but is merely the expression by learned men of a state of things which the evolution of society has actually brought about. The attempt, therefore, to apply the maxims, mostly pedantic, of Western law to a condition of international society which is the outgrowth of milleniums of contention in an opposite quarter of the globe, is about as sensible as it would have been a century ago to have forced top-boots and ruffles on the Eastern people, or as it would be at the present day to impose on the Chinese military conscription, vote by ballot or the Chicago Convention. The thing is incongruous; its effect is to fill the air with cobwebs which irritate and confuse, but cannot effectually obstruct the penetration of the light or the free operation of natural forces.

Besides, even in the West, where the system of doctrine which passes under the misnomer of international "law" is in its native element, it is a very platonic affair whenever it stands in the way of the interest or the ambitions of any one State. Even when concreted into specific treaties the international obligation will always be subordinate to the interest of the country. The treaty of Versailles will not for a single day defer the invasion of France by Germany, or of Germany by France; and the Treaty of Berlin does not hinder Russian agents from plotting in Bulgaria, nor does it enable Austro-Hungary to dispense with a single squadron of cavalry. This so-called international law could not even bear the strain of such an eminently pacific affair as the Geneva Arbitration, but was obliged to accommodate its principles to the foregone arbitrary conclusions of that august tribunal.

How much more then is it a mockery of common sense to attempt to regulate the attitude of China towards her neighbours by academical formulae, which are of little more effect in their native soil than the voting of a Young Men's Debating Society.

Nothing is easier than to point out inconsistencies and even contradictions in the conduct of China toward her tributaries. It is a string which we are tired of harping on. But when all is said the practical question remains untouched. China as a nation has the instinct of self-preservation which must command respect, and though she has made many grievous blunders, through ignorance, in following that instinct she has not thereby forfeited her rights to maintain at least what is left to her. The Corean question is for China not a question for learned research, but one of vital import. We have on a former occasion likened it to the relation between England and Ireland; and we think the analogy is good. Whatever the feeling of the people may be, and whatever history may say, China can no more allow Corea to become the lodgment of an invader than England can Ireland; and those who are plotting for the independence of Corea are either very innocent or they are consciously planning an easy scheme of invasion of China. For no man, who is not carried off the solid ground by some strong inflation, can possibly regard the independence of a country placed as Corea is as a possible solution of her aspirations.

And yet it must be confessed that the best of causes may be ruined by bad agencies and mistaken methods. China in her intercourse with foreigners has always resorted to the most unfortunate means to gain her ends, which have always resulted in her utter discomfiture. She is too clever by half, and her wonderfully interwoven but essentially puerile intrigues have in every important case turned to her own damage. So it has been, and still is in Corea. China when called upon to assume suzerainty, refused. When called upon to relinquish it, she again refused. She was so astute that she would have the benefit of both positions, while compromised by neither. With her fatuous faith in her capacity to "manage" affairs she flattered herself that she could guide her policy, without reckoning with the external forces which she herself had called into existence. Consequently, every single step taken with the exception of the placing of the Customs in the tried hands of the Inspector-General has been a blunder, from the despatch of Commodore Shufeldt with a draft treaty in 1881 till the qualified permission to the Corean Government to send representatives abroad in 1887. There is not a rock or shoal on which the Chinese could have struck which they have avoided. For whatever happens in Corea China is responsible, for, although disasters will be caused proximately by the intriguing and unprincipled foreigners now in the country, it is the fault of China that they are there, and that they are in a position to make mischief.

Of all the blunders, however, which China has committed, perhaps the most serious has been the selection of her representatives in Corea, and, to narrow the proposition down to strictly contemporary history, worst of all has been the continuance in office of the present Resident at Seoul. A man of inferior rank to begin with, an inexperienced youth, and one of the brusque breed of Chinese officials like the famous Chang-pei-lun of Tsung-li Yamen and Foochow Arsenal notoriety, Yuen's conception of his duties seems to have been to hector and harass the King on every occasion; to meddle and muddle in affairs which were no concern of his; and generally to carry things with a high hand. As a natural consequence, these proceedings have turned the hearts of loyal Coreans bitterly against China, have alienated the sympathies of foreigners, and have deprived China of those sentimental alliances which are so important in national affairs. People say, and not unnaturally, anything is better than the tyrannical *regime* of the Representative of China. The Corean people have to be considered, and it is nothing to them whether their King owns China or some more civilized power as suzerain; but it is a great deal to them to be the victims of the caprices of a Chinese Taotai and to escape a present and pressing evil the King, the nobles, and people alike, are probably willing to incur the risk of a greater which is uncertain and remote.

The welfare of a small State must, even on the principle of poetical justice, give way to that of a large one, and neither the chronic misman-agement of China nor the outraged feelings of the Coreans are sufficient to deprive the Chinese State of its natural rights, which are based on the primitive duty of self-preservation. But there is no denying that the injudicious proceedings of China must create difficulties for the foreign powers which would naturally be disposed to lend their moral support to her in the maintenance of her position; much as the rights of Turkey over her tributaries were upset by the current of antagonism which was set in motion by the "atrocities" which were laid to the charge of her officials. Whether it be possible for China to reconsider her treatment of the Corean kingdom, and by replacing the energetic Yuen by a representative of high rank and of conciliatory disposition to undo the damage which has been done, and gain the goodwill and confidence of the Corean Government, is more than we can say. But it is the very first step towards the amelioration of the present strained relations between the countries. No doubt the foreign intriguers, and those who have honestly persuaded themselves that they are doing a noble thing in fighting for the oppressed, would exert all their feverish energies to prevent any friendly *rapprochement* between the vassal and the suzerain. But foreign governments, as apart from the vain and puffed up individuals in question, have also their serious responsibilities in the matter. Great as the faults of China have been in the treatment of her tributaries, it should be remembered, in mitigation of guilt, that those on which we have laid stress are all the result of her having to deal with a state of circumstances which was new to her, and which was entirely brought about by the action of foreign nations. Had they kept away, China and Corea could have gone on for centuries probably without any friction or trouble, but foreigners come on the scene and with very little reason or justification they demand that Corea shall be opened. Thus this poor country has been dragged into the light of day, and a horde of busybodies let loose on the Court, setting up agitations; and then China is required to define with the academical precision of Grotius, Wheaton, or Vattel, her relationship to the Corean State. For the inevitable confusion resulting from this forced situation the foreign powers are primarily responsible, and their honour is involved in minimizing the effects of their aggressiveness to the utmost of their power.

ARTICLE 3

Mr. Denny's Pamphlet[3]

We do not intend, at present at least, to enter into any minute discussion upon the various issues—some much envenomed—raised in the pamphlet written by Mr. O. N. Denny, copies of which have been sparingly circulated, so that a *brochure* cannot yet be considered as a document before the public for consideration and debate. We have, however, seen a copy, and regret that Mr. Denny, impelled by anger, and reckless of consequences to the ruler he desires to serve, has committed the grave error of issuing such an inflammatory document.

In 1885 Mr. Denny, whose honourable career here and in Shanghai as Consular representative of the United States brought him into close contact with the Viceroy Li [Li Hung-chang], for whom indeed he very frequently expressed not only high admiration but strong personal attachment, was invited to become advisor to the King and Government of Corea, and in July 1885 accepted the post. The choice appeared to be fortunate in all its circumstances. Yuen [Yuan Shih-k'ai] warmly approved, so that no fear of jealousy on the part of the Chinese Envoy existed. Mr. Denny was trusted by the Chinese Government, and had the support and amity of the Viceroy, and all foreign residents, including the representatives of Russia and Japan, welcomed it. Everything promised well.

Before Mr. Denny left Tientsin to take up his post in Seoul, he received short and plain instructions for his guidance from the Viceroy Li. Mr. Denny was the nominee of China to serve the Corean King and Government. He was to uphold the *status quo* of Corea *vis-a-vis* to China; he was to advise the Corean Government and the Chinese Resident upon all matters that required reference to a Western counsellor; he was to promote sound progress, provided Corea could bear the charges and was ripe for the innovation, but was to avoid aught that would embarrass the feeble finances; he was to report to the Viceroy when necessary, and was to count on the help of China, which earnestly desired the welfare of her tributary.

Mr. Denny was received at Seoul by both the Court and Yuen with open arms, but ere long differences of opinion arose which ended in a bitter quarrel between him and the Chinese Envoy, a quarrel never since healed. From that time of the quarrel Mr. Denny, not finding the support he expected, has become estranged from Chinese interests, has renounced his former friendship for the Viceroy, has done all he could to induce Corea to break away from allegiance to China; finally, after many stormy incidents, and much pressure on the Viceroy, the dispute has become intensified, and Mr. Denny, to justify his courses, has issued the pamphlet to which we refer.

The brochure, which contains 30 pages, narrates briefly the circumstances of his appointment, complains of constant opposition from Chinese officials, accuses the Viceroy of failing to keep promises, and then in about 15 pages discusses and opposes the Chinese claim of suzerainty over Corea. We do not deem Mr. Denny's contention to be worthy of his legal reputation, as his arguments are in most cases not apposite to the question at issue, which has a firm historical basis. In our paper of the 8th inst. we reprinted a translation of the Manchu records, dealing with the story of the substitution of the Manchu suzerainty for that of the Mings, which existed previously, and in our paper of the 15th inst. we presented to our readers the impartial testimony of the Abbé Dallet, drawn from Corean archives, and which, as we have since found, are confirmed by Mr. Griffis, the latest historian of Corea. We also adduced the frank declarations of Corean officials to Mr. Oppert. These proofs of suzerainty, existing from ancient times till now unbroken, authoritatively confute Mr. Denny's references to Wheaton and others, and citations from Western international law, which do not apply to Chinese and Corean affairs even theoretically.

On page 16 Mr. Denny deals with the motives for sending Corean envoys to foreign States, and the injustice of the limitations made by the Peking Government. It is, however, now plain, even to the Corean Government, the missions were foolish in origin, and it is well that they proved abortive. Foreign nations, with but one serious exception, rather desire the *status quo* between China and Corea should endure than otherwise, while Corea has no foreign interests, even of a trivial kind, and the charges of the missions were a serious burden upon a bankrupt treasury. The missions were the result of unworthy intrigues, and it is well their failure has been ignominious.

In page 19 Mr. Denny begins to formulate a series of charges against Yuen, the Chinese Resident, all grave, and culminating in a passionate accusation of a complicated crime, involving treason, arson, and murder. We discuss the charges in their order.

As regards the seeming arrogance and oppressiveness of Yuen in his bearing towards the Corean King and Court, Mr. Denny may have much reason for his charges, and yet Yuen may have valid justifications. Yuen is a young man of much ability; hardy, fearless, ready to assume responsibility for his acts, and, what is rare among Chinese officials, willing, when occasion demands, to take the initiative. He had strong claims on the King. When, in the last bloody revolt, the King's Ministers were cut down, the King a prisoner and in fear of his life, and the Queen in hiding, with murderers searching for her and intending to kill her, Yuen summoned the Chinese troops, took prompt and skillful military action, saved both King and Queen, quelled the revolt, and averted anarchy. He counted, perhaps, on some grateful remembrance of his services, and for a time was highly favoured. All things went well between King, Government, and Resident till Mr. Denny appeared. Yuen then felt he was in disfavour, and for more than two years has had to bear incessant opposition, studied affront, the hostile intrigues of the foreign adventurers who have wrought so much mischief in the feeble Court, and all signs of enmity of which malignant foes are capable. Small room for wonder that Yuen, a man of hot and fierce temper, has gradually become exasperated, and that for a long time there has been no semblance of goodwill and but little outward courtesy between Court and Resident.

In page 20 a charge of smuggling is stated, which may be true, as Chinese, whether in merchant vessels or warships, are prone to it. It is a very common offence in China. The use of Yuen's seal, on the occasion referred to, might have occurred without his knowledge, and we can, knowing how fraudulent papers have been stamped here with genuine official seals, believe the fact and yet exculpate Yuen.

In pages 21 and 22 Mr. Denny announces a grave charge of criminal and even murderous conspiracy of which Yuen is said to have been guilty, and with the complicity of the Viceroy Li. The nature of the charge is that a plot was formed to depose the King, and to confine or exile him, to declare as heir-apparent his nephew, and to carry on a long Regency under the Dai-in-Kun, who is father of the King. The plot narrated involved very serious crimes and, probably, much bloodshed.

We entirely disbelieve the story. When we first learnt the nature of Mr. Denny's specific charge we were disposed to consider there must have been some basis for it as concerned Yuen, and no doubt there were plots and counter plots, but subsequent inquiries, involving matters not yet ripe for publication, force us to conclude the accusation, as regards Yuen and the Viceroy, is unfounded. That either should have acted, as stated, is rather impossible than improbable. We dismiss the charge against Yuen, and, consequently, the Viceroy Li, as wholly unworthy of credence, even if only for one reason, which is all powerful with Chinese officials. The King of Corea is tributary and vassal, receives investiture from the Chinese Emperor—his suzerain—so that no Chinese official would for one moment dare to give passive sanction much less active aid to any plot that would involve change or modification of the succession to the Corean Kingdom, as such a proceeding implies treason against the Dragon Throne. It will be recollected that in the Taiping and Nienfei rebellions scarcely an official, and not one man of rank, ever joined the revolters, an apposite fact deserving recall when debating Mr. Denny's statements. But in any case, if Yuen had allied himself to conspirators against the King, even without actual complicity in the definite crimes charged, and the Viceroy Li was suspected of siding with Yuen in a disloyal course, the King had ready to his hands a short, simple, and effective means of obtaining reparation for himself and the punishment of Yuen. That this means was not used, and that the charge was confided to Mr. Denny's care is, to us, ample proof of the baselessness of the accusation. The King by right, by historical prescription, could in the circumstances narrated by Mr. Denny, have memorialized the Emperor in the firm assurance that the charge would have been investigated, that justice would have been rendered promptly, and that the Court of Peking had, as always has been the case, the most benevolent regard for its vassal.

On page 25 Mr. Denny tells the failure of the Corean Government to obtain the Viceroy Li's sanction—a proof of the existence of suzerainty—to open Ping-an [P'yŏngyang]. Three ports are now open to trade, and for the closure of Ping-an, which is near the frontier, there are, we understand, political and strategic reasons affecting China as well as Corea, not necessary to discuss now. Mr. Denny shows by his protests that he is imperfectly acquainted with the subject. The rest of the book contains references to the general misconduct of Yuen, and vindicates the King from imputations of weakness and incapacity.

If the pamphlet was designed to promote the welfare of Corea it has signally failed. The publication, showing as it does unreasonable and violent animus, will be like the opening of Pandora's box. It will, we fear, precipitate the advent of questions, not yet ripe for settlement, questions whose solution, in the interests of humanity, had best be relegated to calmer times, because so full of explosive elements.

ARTICLE 4

Glimpses of Corea[4]

The pictures from far Corea, which we publish this week, derive, in addition to their intrinsic interest, a certain timeliness from an international episode which is just now a subject of discussion. We refer to the case of Judge Denny, the American diplomat who, as confidential adviser to the King of Corea, has contrived to render himself a *persona non grata* with the Chinese Government. China exercises a nominal suzerainty over Corea, and it was Li Hung Chang, the Chinese Prime Minister, who appointed Judge Denny as special commissioner at the court of the Corean King. The United States Government is in no way concerned in the matter. Judge Denny's offense appears to have been something like that of the late British Minister at Washington, having consisted in the writing of a letter, or memorial, to Senator Mitchell, of Oregon, in which the *status* of Corea was elaborately discussed, and the policy of China in that quarter criticised with some asperity. The Chinese Premier makes the graver charge that his *protégé* has treacherously lent his influence to the intrigues of the Russians, who are at present endeavoring to intrench themselves in Corea.

This episode indicates the unsettled political condition of the so-called "Land of the Morning Calm," where two incipient revolutions have been quelled during the past decade, and a third was threatened last Summer. At the bottom of all the trouble, in reality, lies the rivalry of Russia and Great Britain in the Far East. The former Power apparently has the upper hand in Corea, a treaty having been signed last September assuring the country of Russia's protection in case of necessity.

Corea has a population of 15,000,000 people; and the City of Seoul, though not the largest in the kingdom, has been the capital ever since the present dynasty came into power, nearly 500 years ago. It was selected for its location, affording as it does a well-drained basin of granite sand, surrounded by hills and mountains, so joined by the several ridges as to form almost a complete amphitheatre, ten miles in circumference. These adjoining mountains afford numerous strong natural fastnesses, which are provided with artificial fortifications where necessary, and are kept constantly garrisoned and provisioned as places of retreat for the royal family in times of danger.

The main thoroughfares of the City of Seoul are some two hundred feet broad, and are usually clean though crowded, but the more distinctively residence streets are not over twenty feet wide as a rule. As they are crowded with travel and lined with the houses of the poor, they are apt to be untidy and not very attractive. On these streets, aside from the occasional large gate leading into a gentleman's establishment, there is little evidence of respectability to be seen, for even the front of a gentleman's residence is given up to servant's quarters, and is allowed to look as shabby as it will, as there is no attempt at street display.

"About nine o'clock every evening," writes an American resident, "the deep, rich tones of a bell are heard throughout the capital; they come from a little pagoda in the centre of the city, which holds a large bell some twelve or fifteen feet in height. Formerly, after the ringing of this 'curfew,' the men disappeared from the streets, which were then given up to the women, who flit about with their little lanterns from house to house, listening to and relating the gossip that is as dear to them as to their sisters on the other side of the world. They enjoy their freedom, even if they must be creatures of the night, and a night is never so stormy but a few of these fair ones may be seen by the privileged official, or foreigner, who may chance to be upon the streets. Recently, however, the law compelling men to leave the streets after the ringing of the bell has been repealed, owing to the fact that so many outrages were committed that it was thought to be a safeguard to allow all men upon the streets, that the honest might be present to answer cries of help and defend the women against the unprincipled. After the ringing of this bell the city-gates are closed, amid the weird blasts of native buglers, and a very great quiet then settles over the dark city."

Mr. Denny on Corean Affairs[5]

A couple of days since one of our staff had an interview with Mr. O. N. Denny, Adviser to the King of Corea, and Director of Foreign Affairs. Mr. Denny from his previous residence at the U.S. Consulate-General, is so well-known to most of our readers, that it is unnecessary to preface his remarks with the usual description of his personal appearance. After a mild and good natured protest against the categorical interview, as an institution, of which, the Reporter reminded him, Mr. Denny's countrymen were the responsible patentees, Mr. Denny said he had no objection to speak, on Corean affairs, which he proceeded to do without much appearance of reserve, save upon one or two personal points, and with great fluency of speech, and earnestness. The first part of the conversation was in a large measure made up of a justification of his pamphlet, which Mr. Denny said he was forced to write to explain his attitude towards the Chinese resident Yuan [Yuan Shih-k'ai] and to place the outside world in possession of the latter's overbearing and blustering conduct towards the Corean Government. Mr. Denny expressed himself very forcibly upon the subject of Yuan's misconduct and attitude towards an independent King, who although a tributary of the Emperor of China, is [not], said he, and never has been a vassal of this empire. "But my chief wish in the line which I have taken" said the King's Adviser "is to preserve the good feeling and harmony between China and Corea which have always existed till the present time, and have now only been interrupted by the unfortunate and unbearable conduct of the Representative Yuan." Mr. Denny laid great emphasis upon the fact that his position towards China, notwithstanding his championing the cause of the "Hermit Kingdom" was as cordial and friendly as ever, while his feelings towards the Viceroy of Chihli [Li Hung-chang] were quite as cordial as before the present straining of the relations, between the two countries. Proceeding further into the subject of the natural connection between China and Corea, Mr. Denny's language was even more unmistakable, and he spoke of the close bond of intimacy which had during the past, drawn the two countries together, Corea having drawn largely upon China for her laws, religion, manners, and customs, while the sympathies of the two peoples have always been in common, and the language of Korea to-day is the language of China of a thousand years ago. "But" pursued Mr. Denny "although everything points to the closest intimacy and friendliness between China and her peninsular neighbour, who it is true has signed a tributary treaty with the Emperor, China has no earthly right to claim, under international laws or usage, or their historical relations, vassalage from Corea, which has ever jealously preserved, and will I hope, be ever able to preserve her independence and freedom from interference in her domestic as well as international policy, by her more powerful neighbour." In proof of this assertion Mr. Denny reverted to the several treaties which Corea has concluded with European powers, and with the United States, in which it was expressly stated in the preamble that Corea was an independent state. "I am sorry to say" said Mr. Denny "that in her struggle with the tyrannical and violent Chinese Representative at Seoul, Corea has had her motives misconstrued, and her position *vis a vis* China misstated by the foreign press in China and Japan.["] Mr. Denny as a case in point, referred to erroneous, and misleading statements in the *Chinese Times* that a treaty of vassalage was concluded between Corea and a Manchu prince in 1637. "Now this is erroneous" said Mr. Denny. "The treaty by which the writer endeavours to place Corea in a false position, was concluded in 1636 with a prince in open rebellion against the then ruling dynasty; and under no rule of international law that I have ever read, can it be construed into a treaty of vassalage to China. It was ten years anterior to the wresting of the Chinese throne from the Mings by the Manchu dynasty that this treaty was concluded with a Manchu prince. Japan might as well claim Corea as a vassal state, because Corea was some couple of hundred years ago in the habit of sending tribute to the Tycoon. Nor has there ever been, since 1636, any treaty made with China that by any possibility of reasoning could be twisted into a treaty of Corea's vassalage."

In reply to a question as to the genuine reason for the recent despatch of embassies to foreign Courts by Corea, Mr. Denny said ["]the King had full powers, as he had to make foreign treaties, to send ministers abroad, but when it reached the ears of Yuan that such a step was about to be taken he instantly set himself against it, and endeavoured to frighten the King by threats and by every means in his power, from doing what as an independent sovereign, he has a perfectly legal right to do, as I have endeavoured to show in my pamphlet. But the obstructive and threatening action of Yuan had only the effect of confirming the King in his determination to send his representatives to Western Courts."

"What do you think of the Russian intrigues in the Capital, will they amount to much?" the reporter asked. "I do not believe very much in them. I do not for a moment imagine that Russia would undertake the responsibility of establishing a protectorate over Corea, and incur the enmity of China. Russia is all for conciliating China for the purpose of developing overland trade. Besides the difficulty of governing a people like the Coreans, with little or no sympathy with Western methods, would be enormous, and every order would have to be enforced at the point of the bayonet perhaps. Such a move would at once turn the eyes of the Coreans with regret and longing towards China, from which the conduct of Yuan just now is calculated to turn them away. I know that a few years ago a desperate attempt was made to bring about such a consummation, but it did not succeed, happily both for Corea and Russia. To such a policy I shall always offer my most strenuous objection, nor do I think that the King would ever be so foolish as to be led into such a mistake. What is aimed at is Corean autonomy, the right for Corea to manage her own affairs at home and abroad and to develope the natural [re]sources of the country. I have great confidence in the future of Corea. She is naturally a very rich country, but it would be foolish to imagine that all her resources can be availed of before several years to come.["] But that there is an era of prosperity before the country Mr. Denny thought was clearly shown by the recent Customs returns, although the revenue from the exports, so far, has not compared favourably with that from imports. "The King," said Mr. Denny "is most anxious to see his dominions enriched by foreign trade and intercourse, but until the present political complications are disposed of he can do very little." On the subject of the statement recently published in the *Mainichi Shimbun* and reproduced by some of the foreign papers in Japan, to the effect that his life had been several times threatened of late, Mr. Denny said he was not afraid of any danger of that sort, and the story was an invention which was suggested to some ingenious scribe by his (Mr. Denny's) peculiar position in Corea. Speaking of the policy of Japan in Seoul, Mr. Denny said that since the treaty with Corea in 1876, the Japanese seemed to be directing all their efforts to the acquisition of commercial advantages and trade, and by friendly intercourse sought to wipe out the painful recollections on the part of the Coreans, of the last great invasion of their country by one of the Tycoons.

As to the ulterior aims in Corea of the Russian Government, Mr. Denny, once more expressed himself as a non-believer in the general opinion that the great object of the Czar's representatives in the Far East is still to extend their territory by the annexation or protectorate of Corea. Mr. Denny went even further in this direction, he gave it as his deliberate opinion that no western power, without the greatest expense, trouble, responsibility and sacrifice of life could obtain a paramount position in Corea. He thought that some kind of settlement was now approaching, and the sooner it came the better it would be for all parties. As far as he himself was concerned, what he was striving for was an amicable agreement with China, and a speedy return to the old paths of amity and harmony between the two countries. This, however, was not what the Chinese Representative by any means desired to see. Yuan is a military mandarin, with the smattering of military education after a fashion, and with an unlimited and unfortunate belief in the creed of force as a panacea for all political ills. His object all along had been to excite and foment disturbance in Seoul, his leading idea being to come in with a Chinese Army and carry everything before him by force of arms. This was what Mr. Denny strove to avert. The Coreans did not aim at results through the force of arms. His Majesty, according to Mr. Denny's opinion, is a long way in advance of most of his subjects in progressive ideas, and is anything but the vacillating and weak character which he is often represented to be. Strange as it may seem Mr. Denny does not speak Corean,—only a few words—and carries on his business with the King through an interpreter. One thing of importance which the reporter elicited in the interview was the fact that the commercial treaty between Russia and Corea which we recently reprinted from a Japanese paper, and of which no confirmation has hitherto transpired, may be regarded as authentic. It was signed a couple of months ago by the President of the Council and Mr. Denny on behalf of Corea, and M. Waeber, the Russian Minister at Seoul, and it has been or is about to be ratified. By this treaty important privileges are given to Russian traders in Corea, but there is no great political significance in that, said Mr. Denny, as all the other powers can claim the same privileges under the favoured nations clause. Mr. Denny is a firm believer in the auriferous wealth of Corea, and believes that when the present placer mining is superseded by better methods of extraction, the amount of gold produced will be enormously increased. An even surer source of wealth he believes also exists in the great timber tracts in the North of the Peninsula, which even now exports large quantities of valuable wood to China, and in conclusion he expressed himself sanguine of Corea's future prosperity, if she succeeds in getting fair treatment from China, and freeing herself from the pernicious influence of the Chinese Representative.

ARTICLE 6

Korea Kingless[6]

Washington, Dec. 29.—Diplomatic circles are very much excited over a rumor that has gained currency within the past few days, which, in some quarters, is taken to foreshadow no less an event than the dissolution of the kingdom of Korea, and its final rehabilitation as an absolutely dependent province of China.

The present state of affairs is said to have been brought about by the machinations of Li Hung Chang, the shrewd and far-seeing viceroy of China.

The story is one of continued financial embarrassment at home and of encroachment and unwarranted interference from the outside.

So great has been the constant annoyance and so wearing the continual strain that the present King of Corea has announced his intention of abdicating the throne, leaving it with an empty treasury and an impoverished and shabby royal menage to some other ambitious Celestial, who may be willing to spend his existence, harassed by poverty on the one side and diplomatic intrigue on the other.

At present a trusted emissary of the King is at Hong Kong in consultation with the exiled Corean prince, Min Yun Ik [Min Yŏng-ik], in whose favor the King wishes to abdicate.

The latest advices indicate that Min Yun Ik does not look with favor upon the plan, and the best informed diplomats here are of the opinion that his past experience[s] in rebelling against Chinese authority are still vivid enough in his recollection to prevent him from accepting the offer of the King of a threadbare and heavily mortgaged throne.

The present financial straits of the King of Korea [have] been brought about largely through the inability of the customs officials of the little kingdom to collect their own revenues.

For many years the country of Korea has maintained a sort of quasi independence of China, but it has been the independence of the mouse which runs at liberty within easy reach of the cat's paw. Let it take a step beyond certain limits and it is brought up with a round turn.

When the question of China's responsibility for overt acts committed by Korean subjects has been raised, the entire independence of the little kingdom has been tacitly admitted by the Chinese office. Indeed, there is now on file at [the] State Department a document in Chinese in which any responsibility for the transgressions of the Koreans is emphatically disavowed by the Chinese government.

Notwithstanding this fact, China still holds Korea as a tributary province, managing and collecting its customs revenue, annually issuing trade regulations for Korea, keeping a so-called commissioner and for some time a regiment of soldiers at Seoul.

The customs policy of Li Hung Chang has materially reduced the revenues of the King of Korea until his exchequer is now comparatively empty, and the prospects for the future without a ray of encouragement.

The Korean legation here, if such it may be called, is slowly but surely sinking out of sight. Of the dozen or more gorgeously attired officials who arrived in the suite of Minister Pak Chung Yung nearly two years ago not one remains.

At the legation of 13th street there is a lonely charge d'affaires, Ye Wan Yong, and his secretary, Ye Cha Yan. All the rest have gone home.

Minister Pak went some time ago. He complained of "ill-health." The others followed in his train, and the present officials were sent out to take the place of the elaborate retinue that left Korea for the United States on board an American man-of-war in the winter of 1887-8.

The embassy came to this country against the protest of the Emperor of China, and though Korea professes to be entirely independent of the Flowery Kingdom, Minister Pak remembers that Min Yun Ik, a wealthy and influential Korean who had been unfortunate enough to incur the displeasure of the Chinese government, was banished to the Bonin islands. No force was used. He was simply told to go and he went.

When the King of Korea decided to send an embassy to the United States, the State Department instructed the admiral of the Asiatic squadron to convey the embassy to Yokohama, where they would embark for San Francisco; the United States steamer Omaha, Capt. McNair, was ordered to Chemulpoo from Nagasaki.

When the vessel arrived Capt. McNair learned that Minister Pak, upon receiving notice of his appointment, had taken to the woods. For several weeks expeditions were sent off from the ships each day to hunt for the minister, but in vain. One afternoon Minister Pak came down to the coast. When the boats came off for him, Pak and his retainers stood watching the billows with undisguised terror. They had never before seen the ocean.

They were hustled aboard in short order, but the Omaha was hardly a mile from shore when six vessels of the Chinese squadron hove in sight. They had been sent to Chemulpoo to prevent the departure of Minister Pak, but arrived too late. The Omaha fired a vice-admiral's salute and steamed right through the squadron. The Chinese were so astonished that the Omaha was nearly hull down before the salute was returned. If the Chinese admiral had arrived a half hour sooner, nothing could have induced Minister Pak to embark for America.

For the past year the Korean officials have in many instances omitted the formality of paying American employees, and when they have made remittances it has been in silver, a large part of which frequently proved to consist of bad Mexican dollars.

Not long ago Capt. Lee and Maj. Cummins, who were induced to go to Korea to reorganize the army, became so clamorous for their salaries that the Korean officials broke their contracts by dismissing them without paying the arrears of salary.

These facts were immediately communicated to Mr. Blaine, who less than a fortnight ago cabled Minister Dinsmore to make the most emphatic demand for the payments of all moneys due Lee and Cummins.

It is expected that these officers will reach Washington early in

January. It is a problem as to whether the other Americans in the king's employ will receive a dollar of the money they have earned.

Wiley Li Hung Chang, who was referred to as being as acute an observer as Gen. Grant, and as a statesman the equal in every respect of Bismarck, has been greatly amused by all this comedy, and particularly the part the so-called Korean legation has played in America.

It has been a part of the more or less intelligent diplomatic theory of the United States government, to maintain an out and out legation and ministry resident in Korea, and to keep a man-of-war almost constantly stationed at Chemulpoo.

England, Russia, France and Germany, who play a diplomatic game well, and the two first alone having nothing to lose or gain, have kept only consul generals at Seoul, giving them, temporarily, the rank of charge de affaires. All these charges received their instructions from their respective ministers at Pekin.

From the present outlook it may not be many months before United States Minister Dinsmore finds his occupation gone. In the event that Korea resolves itself once more into a dependent province of China, ministers of any sort at Seoul would hardly be a personal gratae to His Excellency Li Hung Chang.

A. Maurice Low

Appendix B
China and Korea

by O. N. Denny,
Advisor to the King, and Director of
Foreign Affairs[1]

A vacancy having occurred in the position of Foreign Advisor to the King of Korea, and Inspector of Customs, and His Majesty having requested His Excellency Li Chung Tang [Li Hung-chang], Viceroy of Chihli, to procure the services of another, I was in July 1885 invited to the post. I entered upon the duties of Advisor—the Customs' branch of the position having been placed under the Customs of China before my arrival in the East—with the assurance that in my efforts to preserve peace and good order, and in all that pertained to the prosperity of Korea, I should have the cordial support of the Viceroy,—an assurance which, I regret to say, has not been verified. On the contrary, from the very first, I have met with almost every conceivable kind of opposition from Chinese sources. The failure of the Viceroy to keep his promise in this regard, I am at a loss to understand, unless it is due to the Peking Government's disapproval of his Korean policy. In view of this and the fact that China's course seems so unwarrantable and unjust, as well as against the best interest of Korea and China, I determined to avail myself of the present occasion to publicly point out—all efforts of a private character having failed—the dangerous ground China is trying to occupy, and to present Korea's side of the controversy, with a view to correcting, if possible, some of the accepted fallacies on the situation in the peninsular Kingdom and its relations with the Celestial Empire, which have been so often misrepresented in the native, and some of the foreign, newspapers in China for the past two or three years, through design or under a misapprehension of the law as well as the facts. In doing this, the harsher the criticisms may appear, the more it is to be regretted that they are merited. First.—I shall notice China's claim to vassal or dependent relations with Korea. Second.—The former's treatment of her so-called vassal. Third.—The charge that the King is weak and unfit to govern the country. And before I have finished, I shall endeavor to show that the former is about as fictitious as the latter is without foundation. As Korea, in the exercise of a right which none but sovereign and independent states possess, concluded a treaty of friendship, navigation, and commerce with Japan, independently of China, and later on with Western countries in accordance with international usage, the rights acquired and the obligations assumed must be determined by the laws which have always governed the enforcement of such compacts. In the light of these defined and well-settled rules, it will be in order to enquire into some of the rights, powers, and responsibilities of a sovereign state, and how vassal relations are established, as well as into the duties and obligations a dependent state owes to its suzerain, in order to more clearly determine the political status of Korea.

In general terms, a sovereign or independent state is defined by almost all authors on international jurisprudence to be, any nation or people, whatever the character or form of its constitution may be, which governs itself independently of other nations; while [Henry] Wheaton, who ought to be the best authority in this case, as China has adopted him as her standard author, says:—"sovereignty is the supreme power by which any state is governed: this supreme power may be exercised either internally or externally. Internal sovereignty is that which is inherent in the people of any state or is vested in its ruler by its municipal constitution or fundamental laws. External sovereignty consists in the independence of one political society in respect to all other political societies; and it is by the exercise of this branch of sovereignty that the international relations of one political society are maintained in peace and in war with all other political societies." A nation which has always managed its internal as well as external concerns in its own way, free from the interference or dictation of any foreign power, is juridically independent, and must be ranked in the category of sovereign states. The unerring test, however, of a sovereign and independent state, is its right to negotiate, to conclude treaties of friendship, navigation and commerce, to exchange public ministers, and to declare war and peace with other sovereign and independent powers. These are rights and conditions compatible and consistent with sovereignty which, when possessed by a state, place it in the great family of independent nations; while states which do not possess such powers, must be ranked as semi-independent or dependent according to the expressed terms of the agreement.

An advocate of vassalage, in the *North-China Daily News*, some months ago, in support of his position, used substantially the following language:—"At the end of the 17th and beginning of the 18th centuries the sanction of the Chinese Emperor had to be obtained before the successor chosen by the King of Korea could receive the title of heir-apparent, and then could not assume the title of king until it was conferred on him by Pekin." The correspondent states the case much stronger than the facts warrant. If he had put it in the form of a request, a graceful act by a tributary state, rather than on the basis of an imperative obligation to the Pekin Government, he would have been more in accord with the facts; but whether he over or under stated them makes no material difference, as relations of vassalage were never established by the commands of a superior in exceptional cases or through the deferential acts of an inferior. Liu Kiu, Annam and Burmah, in the history of China's precarious claims to suzerainty over those states, did the same thing, and today the first-named forms a part of the sovereignty of the Empire of Japan, the second belongs to the Republic of France, while the third recently passed to the sovereign control of Great Britain. Wheaton on the law of nations states the case infinitely stronger against the correspondent than the latter does in favor of China's contention, when he says, "The sovereignty of a particular state is not impaired by its occasional obedience to the commands of other states or *even the habitual influence exercised by them over its councils*. It is only when this obedience or this influence *assumes the form of express compact* that the sovereignty of the state inferior in power is legally affected by its connection with the other." John Austin, a modern writer of considerable celebrity on international law, in one of his able lectures, delivered in London in 1873, states the case with equal clearness when he says, "A feeble state holds its independence precariously or at the will of the powerful states to whose aggressions it is obnoxious, and since it is obnoxious to its aggressions, it and the bulk of its subjects render obedience to commands which they occasionally express or intimate; but since the obedience and commands are comparatively few and rare, they are not sufficient to constitute the relation of sovereignty and subjection between the powerful states and the feeble state with its subjects. In spite of those commands and in spite of that obedience the feeble state and its subjects are an independent political society whereof the powerful states are not the sovereign portion, although the powerful states are permanently superior, and although the feeble state is permanently inferior there is neither the habit of command nor a habit of obedience on the part of the latter, and although the latter is unable to defend and maintain its independence, *the latter is independent of the former in fact or practice*." The only vassal or dependent relations recognised by the law of nations are those resulting from conquest, international agreement or convention of some kind, and as such relations do not exist between the two countries by virtue of either of these requirements, and in all reasonable probability will never be established by agreement or convention, it remains to be seen whether they will exist in future by conquest.

Korea, however, is a tributary state of China: relations which have been sustained in the past with the utmost good faith, and which Korea desires in all sincerity to continue so long as China's treatment is generous, friendly and just. But the tributary relations one state may hold to another do not and cannot in any degree affect its sovereign and independent rights. For this reason, the tribute annually paid by Korea to China does not impair her sovereignty or independence any more than the tribute now paid by the British Government to China on account of Burmah impairs the sovereign and independent rights of the British Empire, or the tribute formerly paid by the principal maritime powers of Europe to the Barbary states affected the sovereign rights and independence of those European powers. Wheaton says, concerning the Barbary States, that "while they are anomalous in character, yet their occasional obedience to the commands of the Sultan, accompanied with irregular payments of tribute, does not prevent them from being considered by the Christian powers of Europe and America as independent states with whom the international relations of war and peace are maintained on the same footing with other Mohammedan sovereignties." There are good and valid reasons why Korea desires to preserve the traditional relations of close friendship which have so happily existed between the two countries so long. Their geographical positions, under friendly intercourse, make them a source of strength to each other, while the fact that Korea has drawn largely upon China's population, language, religion, laws, education, arts, manners and customs, which have contributed so much to the sum total of Korean civilization, all combine to strengthen the chain of attachment, and cause her to look to China, as in the past, for friendly advice rather than in any other direction; and in my judgment nothing will interrupt this friendship but a continuation of the illegal and high-handed treatment Korea is now receiving at the hands of the Chinese, and their studied and persistent attempts to destroy Korean sovereignty by absorbing the country.

It was due to the faith which the King had in China's professions of friendship for Korea that induced His Majesty, when the advisability of making treaties with Western countries was pressed upon him, to take counsel of the distinguished Viceroy at Tientsin; and I know of my own knowledge that it was due to a similar faith in the King that induced the Chung Tang to advise the establishment of such relations as the surest means of improving the condition of the country and people, as well as preserving the sovereign rights of his kingdom; and later on, when the first of the Western treaties came to be negotiated, which was with America, the Viceroy was invited as the friend of the King, having the broadest experience in such important matters, to assist in the negotiations. Two drafts were submitted to that Convention for consideration, one by the Viceroy and the other by the special envoy [Robert Shufeldt] who conducted the negotiations for the United States. The very first clause in the Viceroy's draft was a demand for the recognition of vassal or dependent relations between China and Korea, which the agent of the U.S. Government declined to consider or even discuss further than to say that, as his mission was to make a treaty of commerce and friendship with an independent state, such a treaty he would make or none at all. Notwithstanding this, the Viceroy urged the approval of this dependent clause to a point beyond which he could not go without breaking off negotiations, when he yielded, and the treaty was then concluded upon the same basis with those of other independent states, and was signed at Chemulpo, May 22nd, 1882. Even if vassalage had been acknowledged in the American treaty by the negotiators, it would not have received the approval either of the U.S. Government or the King of Korea. The next treaty that Korea made was in October following with China, and at the latter's request; and while this treaty has been denominated "rules for the land and water commerce between the trading populations of China and Korea," and while there is the usual mystification and vagueness pervading it that characterizes all of China's intercourse with the peninsular Kingdom, yet it comes nearer being a treaty of friendship, navigation, and commerce than anything else, as I shall endeavor to point out further on.

Treaties with other countries followed in quick succession in the general tenor of the American one, which were however discussed and concluded, not at Tientsin but in Seoul, without reference to the Viceroy or the Chinese Government. Had the relation of suzerain and vassal existed between the two countries, in accord with international jurisprudence, at the time the American treaty was made, does anyone at all versed in public affairs suppose that the Viceroy would have tried so hard to procure its acknowledgment by a friendly power in a public treaty? No, the attempt was based solely on the utter weakness of the contention, which no one appreciated more fully than the Viceroy himself. After the ratification of the American treaty, the question of the dependency of Korea, for the moment at least, seems to have been abandoned; at all events, arrangements were at once made for the enforcement of the stipulations of the treaty: ports were opened, a Customs' service established by the King, with inspector, commissioners and a full staff of subordinate officers for the work. Diplomatic representatives were appointed as treaties were ratified, who from time to time presented their credentials and took their respective places at His Majesty's Court in Seoul; and among them was the representative of China, with the title of "His Imperial Majesty's Commissioner" printed on his card, and who was appointed in pursuance of the treaty already referred to. This official continued, in an unassuming way, to represent his Government, upon terms of equality with his colleagues, for more than two years, when he was succeeded by the present Commissioner Yuan [Yuan Shih-k'ai], for supposed meritorious services rendered his Government in the Korean disturbance of 1884, and who, for a short time, followed in the footsteps of his predecessor; but the honor so suddenly thrust upon him seems to have inflated him to such an extent that serious consequences might have resulted to him had not his indiscreet enthusiasm found vent in the resurrection of the dependency scheme, which, for the credit of his Government, ought never again to have come to the surface; for, if the conclusion of the Japanese and American treaties upon the basis of Korean independence—every article of the latter having been approved by the Viceroy, followed by similar treaties with the leading powers of Europe, and China having shared in their practical operations for two and a-half years—did not honorably settle it, the question ought finally to have disappeared when the Li-Ito Convention adjourned, by the terms of which China disposed of whatever right she had left—without the consent of Japan—to send troops to Korea, the only means, as a last resort, every independent nation possesses of enforcing its sovereign rights when they are assailed or called in question.

Some time in 1885, after I had been invited to Korea but before my arrival, a policy of absorption, gradual or otherwise, seems to have been decided upon by the Pekin Government. The position of Advisor to the King and Inspector of Customs was segregated, and the Customs' service passed to the control and direction of the Chinese service, under the plausible assurance that it would be better and more economically administered, and that there was no political significance to be attached to the change; and, while the service has been honestly and well adminis-tered under the change, yet no one act, since the conclusion of the treaties, has contributed so much to mislead the public mind in regard to the true relations existing between China and Korea politically, as this ill-advised one on the part of the Korean Government. Neither in the meanwhile was Commissioner Yuan idle, for it was about this time that he adopted as a title for his Legation that miserable misnomer and subter-fuge "Residency," and in the most insolent way claimed to advise and even direct the King in long but empty memorials, and, upon public and official occasions, to assume the role of host instead of guest, on the flimsy pretext that he is "at home" in Korea. But it is asserted that vassalage is distinctly acknowledged by Korea in the treaty sometimes called "the overland trade regulations," above alluded to. Now I assert with much confidence that, if that convention establishes anything so far as this question is concerned, it is exactly the contrary to this. While there are only eight rather lengthy articles in that treaty, yet, as already observed, they cover about all that is necessary in an ordinary treaty of friendship, commerce and navigation. Under the first article China has dispatched her Commissioner with diplomatic powers to Seoul, and consuls to all the open ports to guard the interests of Chinese merchants. The second article yields to China ex[tra]-territorial privileges for her subjects, similar to those enjoyed by the citizens and subjects of the most favored nations. Article third permits the merchant-ships of both countries to visit the open ports of the other, fixes the duties to be paid, provides for relief in case of shipwrecks, regulates the conduct of fishing-vessels, etc. Article fourth permits merchants of either country to visit the open ports of the other, for the purposes of trade, where they may purchase lands and houses, provides tonnage-dues as well as re-export tariff, inhibits trade at the capital of both countries, compels merchants wishing to purchase native produce in the interior to first obtain permits of their consuls, while persons desiring to travel in either country for pleasure, must be provided with passports. Article seventh provides for the dispatch once a month to Korea of a vessel belonging to the China Merchants Company, and permits Chinese men-of-war to repair to the open ports of Korea for the purpose of protecting Chinese consuls and other residents. In the text of this treaty there is not only no reference to vassalage or dependency, but the demands and concessions made exclude the existence of such relations at the time it was concluded. If China believed in the validity of vassal relations, can it be supposed that provisions would have been made for ex[tra]-territorial privileges and passports for Chinese subjects in Korea? Certainly not, for to have done so would have presented the spectacle of a sovereign state demanding ex[tra]-territorial rights and privileges for her own subjects within her own sovereignty, which is the very acme of absurdity. The only reference to vassalage, as interpreted even by the Chinese, is in a preamble, published at the head of this treaty, which may or may not have been in its present form at the time the treaty was signed.

This extraordinary preamble rendered as follows:—"Korea has long been one of *our* vassal states, and in all that concerns rights and observances there are already fixed prescriptions which require no change." Can this be the language of a high joint convention created, not to sign away the sovereign rights of a nation, but to protect them in its intercourse with a neighboring state? It seems rather the *ex-parte* assertion of a fallacy than any proof of the existence of a fact. But the closing paragraph of this preamble, if anything, is still more remarkable. It reads:—"It is understood that the present rules . . . are to be viewed in the light of a favor granted by China to a dependent state, and are not in the category of favored nation treatment applied to other states." Is it a favor to Korea for that state to grant ex[tra]-territorial privileges to the subjects of China while the latter lays claim to suzerainty over the former? Is it a favor to Korea to permit Chinese men-of-war to repair to her open ports to protect Chinese consuls and other residents? And, finally, is it a favor to overrun the Korean capital with Chinese merchants while there is not a Korean merchant in all China? There is an additional reason why this preamble must be erroneous, and that is this: As the Viceroy was one of the plenipotentiaries who concluded the treaty, it is quite out of the range of reason to believe that that distinguished official could have been a party to the assertion that the rules alluded to in the preamble "are not in the category of favored nation treatment applied to other states," for, hardly five months before this, he discussed and sanctioned, as the professed friend of Korea, the 14th Article of the American treaty, which provides that:—"The high contracting powers hereby agree that should at any time the King of Chosen [Korea] grant to any nation or to the merchants or citizens of any nation any right, privilege or favor connected either with navigation, commerce, political or other intercourse which is not conferred by this treaty, such right, privilege or favor shall freely inure to the benefit of the United States, its public officers, merchants and citizens." Not only does the approval of this favored nation clause by the Viceroy destroy the integrity of this part of the preamble alluded to, but what becomes of China's claim to suzerainty over Korea when it is enforced by the treaty powers [?] Would it not irresistibly follow that the latter would have as many suzerains as she has treaties, every one of whose accredited Ministers abroad would have the same right to advise, direct and control the Korean Ministers accredited to other courts in pursuance of those treaties as the Chinese Ministers abroad have?

Nor is this all. For under its enforcement whatever may have been stipulated or may be stipulated between China and Korea—not in the line of favored nation treatment—which is opposed to the spirit or the expressed provisions of the general treaties, or which in any way contravenes the rights, immunities and privileges already vested by such agreements in other powers, either for themselves or for their citizens or subjects, is void and of no effect. But, said the most eminent statesman of the Celestial Empire recently, "Korea is a vassal of China's because upon the conclusion of treaties with Western countries the King gave to the plenipotentiaries who conducted the negotiations autograph letters to be conveyed to the heads of their respective Governments, in which such relations were admitted." Here again I must take issue with the assertion, even though it is made by so eminent a personage as Li Chung Tang. It is true that, just prior to signing the American treaty, an autograph letter was handed down by the King to be delivered with the treaty to the President of the U.S., but that letter admitted nothing more than the King now asserts, namely, that Korea is a tributary state of China, but which, as I have endeavored to point out, does not affect, much less destroys, the sovereign rights of a state, while it asserts in language that cannot be misunderstood the sovereign and independent character which the Korean Government has always maintained, and upon the conditions of which rest all the treaties concluded with Western powers. Subsequent autograph letters given by His Majesty were in effect the same as the first one, so far at least as the relations of Korea to China are concerned. The following is a correct translation of the letter of the King to the President of the U.S.:—

"His Majesty, the King of Chosen, herewith makes a communication. Chosen has been, from ancient times, a state tributary to China; *yet hitherto full sovereignty has been exercised by the Kings of Chosen in all matters of internal administration and foreign relations.* Chosen and the United States, in establishing now by mutual consent a treaty, are dealing with each other upon a basis of equality. The King of Chosen distinctly pledges his own sovereign powers for the complete enforcement in good faith of all the stipulations of the treaty *in accordance with international law.* As regards the various duties which devolve upon Chosen as a *tributary* state to China, with these the U.S. has no concern whatever. Having appointed envoys to negotiate a treaty, it appears to be my duty, in addition thereto, to make this preliminary declaration.

"To the President of the United States.
May 15, 1882."

Whatever interpretation the advocates of the vassalage of Korea may choose to put upon the plain, candid and unmistakeable language contained in the above letter, or however much they may attempt to twist or pervert its meaning, it is perfectly clear that the American Government has given it a construction strictly in accord with its phraseology as well as spirit, for they now hold that, under the treaty of friendship and commerce which accompanied it, the question of Korea's vassalage to China has been definitely settled, so far at least as that Government is concerned. In paragraph 64, Vol. I of [Francis] Wharton's *Digest of International Law of the U.S.* the following language is used by the Government:—"The existence of international relations between the two countries (the U.S. and Korea) as equal contracting parties, is to be viewed simply as an accepted fact," and "the independence of Korea of China is to be regarded by the U.S. as now established." Neither does the American Government stand alone in this regard, for at least two other great powers claiming relations with Korea, equal in importance politically as well as commerically to those claimed by China, insist on maintaining the same sovereignty for Korea that the United States does, while the solemn joint declaration of Japan and Korea, as expressed in the first article of their treaty concluded February 1876, declares that, "Chosen being an independent state, enjoys the same sovereign rights as does Japan, and that their intercourse shall thenceforward be carried on in terms of equality and courtesy." Independently of the treaties which have been made with Korea, the historical relations of that country with China do not admit the existence of any such conditions toward each other as suzerain and vassal. Tributary treaties Korea has signed, but none of vassalage. It has been suggested that Korea signed a treaty in 1636 wherein vassalage was acknowledged. This however is a mistake, as that treaty was also a tributary one, and even then it was in no sense a treaty with China. It was a treaty of capitulation made with a Chinese subject, a Manchu Prince, who was in open rebellion against the Chinese Government and against whom Korea fought on the side of the last Chinese Emperor of the Ming Dynasty, as in 1636 the Mings were still Emperors of China, and no treaty of vassalage was ever signed with them. It was not until 1644, eight years later, that the Manchus ascended the throne at Peking, since which time no vassalage treaty has been signed or agreed to by Korea.

When such relations are held by states in the legal international acceptation of the term, that which disturbs the heart of the sovereign affects the pulse of the vassal, and yet so far as is known neither the wars which have been waged against China by foreign states, nor her rebellions, nor internal dissensions have apparently disturbed or concerned Korea any more than if one nation had been located near the North Pole and the other in the tropics. And yet it was the duty of Korea as a vassal of China to have furnished an army from her hundreds of thousands of soldiers which she has had or could have raised at any stage of her civilization, as well as munitions of war, to aid China in the hour of her greatest need; but not a soldier, gun, or dollar seems to have crossed over from Korea to China for that purpose. In addition to this important fact, if such relations ever existed they ought certainly to have left their imprint on the civilization of Korea, either upon the national emblems, coins, laws, or in some other way, as public notice to other nations of China's responsibility when grievances were to be redressed or wrongs atoned, as well as an acknowledgment on Korea's part of the acceptance of such relations. To those who are versed in international affairs Korea cannot be considered a dependent state, for the reason that the law and the facts have placed her in the column of sovereign and independent states, where she will remain, unless, through the force of superior numbers, she is taken out of it. Korea has the right of negotiation,—a vassal state has not; Korea has concluded treaties of friendship, commerce and navigation with other sovereign and independent states, without reference to China, which a vassal cannot do; and in virtue of those treaties has dispatched public Ministers to the courts of her respective treaty powers, while vassal states cannot even appoint Consuls-General but only Consuls and commercial agents. Korea has the right to declare war or peace, which a vassal cannot do except through its suzerain. China under her treaty is represented at the Korean Court by a diplomatic officer, and by consuls at all the open ports, and when the interests of the Korean Government demand it, they will be similarly represented in China, or friendly intercourse will surely cease to exist between the two Governments. The following language of [Johann Kasper] Bluntschli, a modern international jurist of great clearness, is forcibly applied here. He says:— "Inasmuch as sovereignty tends to unity, such distinctions between vassal sovereignty and sovereign sovereignty cannot subsist long. History shows us the truth of this principle. During the middle ages a number of vassal states existed both in Europe and Asia. To-day they have nearly all disappeared because they have been transformed into sovereign states or have been absorbed by more powerful states. International law ought to keep an account of their development. It ought to respect it. It ought not to contribute to retard it by seeking to perpetuate the unsustainable formalities of an antiquated jurity." International law will keep an account of their development, too, and in its vigilance for the rights of the weak, will keep an account of Korea also in her struggle for the maintenance of independent statehood. After having been by the great nations of the international world literally dragged from the seclusion which had for so many centuries enveloped the little kingdom in mystery, to join the family of civilized nations, under the expressed guarantee of assistance in the event of oppression or unjust treatment, those powers will surely not permit the stultification of this assurance by allowing their younger member to be strangled at the very threshold of its international life.

China's friend and ally Korea desires to be, but her voluntary slave she never will consent to become. The Austro-Hungarian Minister of State, M. Kalnoky, lately said:—"A vassal state in the nineteenth century is an anachronism." However this may be, the time will indeed be sadly out of joint when China succeeds by her peculiar methods in establishing vassalage with Korea; not only so, but when she does a new chapter will have to be added to international jurisprudence, the principles of which such well-known expounders as [Hugo] Grotius, [Emerich de] Vattel and Wheaton never comprehended. . . . At this late date, after China and

Korea having joined the family of nations as sovereign and independent states, and after the former having yielded sovereign control over Korea in the conclusion of treaties, and until recently having acquiesced in the execution of all of the provisions of those treaties, declining responsibility for Korea's conduct at times when responsibility stood for something, and having concluded a treaty with Korea herself, now to claim the existence of dependent relations is not only to abuse language and offend intelligence but it is also an attempt to defy international precedents. Nor is this all, for China's contention becomes even grotesque in character when it is claimed for her that in the discussion and final adjustment of the issue she is above and beyond the range of human reason and long experience, as evinced in the formulation and adoption by the civilised nations of the West of that code of international jurisprudence which has guided those nations so well in the past in their intercourse with each other and by which China, of her own volition, through the conclusion of her treaties consented to be governed and controlled in all of her intercourse with other treaty powers.

But perhaps one of the most careless and inexcusable assertions in relation to this question is the one that the Korean Government admit vassalage without any qualifications whatever, for nothing is further from the truth; and when the King under well-considered advice appointed a Minister to Japan [Min Yŏng-jun], and afterwards the plenipotentiaries to Europe and America [Sim Sang-hak and Pak Chŏng-yang], in order, if possible, to break up the pernicious meddlesomeness of the Chinese with Korean affairs, and which met with such stubborn opposition from the Pekin Government as well as adverse criticism in certain public journals in the East, His Majesty emphasized by that public act his denial of this fallacious statement. Apparently there is no limit to the devices resorted to by the advocates of vassalage. A correspondent of the *Mainichi Shimbun* (Japanese journal) writing to that paper on the 17th of November last, seems to have fallen a victim to one of these, for he says: "It appears that a convention on the appointment by Korea of Ministers to foreign countries has been concluded between her and China and that it consists of the following three articles. 1st.—The Korean Minister of State shall, before sending a Minister abroad, ask advice of the Chinese Minister in Korea. 2nd.—Should the Korean Minister abroad have occasion to communicate with the representative of any other foreign power in the same country on a matter of business, he shall consult with the Chinese Minister in that country. 3rd.—The Korean Minister of State shall, no matter what the official rank of a Minister appointed by them to a foreign country may be, not allow him to take precedence over the Chinese representative in the same country." The only document which could be tortured into anything like the above articles, is the following telegraphic instructions from the Viceroy to Commissioner Yuan, about the 5th of November last. 1st.—"After arriving at his post the Korean representative has to call at the Chinese Legation to ask the assistance of the Minister and to go with the Korean representative to the Foreign Office to introduce him, after which he may call where he likes. 2nd.—If there happen to be festivities at the court, or an official gathering, or any dinner, or the health of someone is drunk, or in meeting together, the Korean representative has always to take a lower place than the Chinese representative. 3rd.—If there happen[s] to be any important or serious question to discuss, the Korean representative has first to consult secretly with the Chinese Minister, and both have to talk over the matter and think together; this rule is compulsory, arising from the dependent relations, but as this does not concern other governments they will not be able to enquire into the matter. At present the question (sending Ministers) has not been decided by Imperial decree. They (the Koreans) have to be advised in a friendly spirit. China and Korea have to cherish for each other feelings of relationship. Ministers are selected from among the Mandarins of reputation, therefore confidence and respect has to be shown them, and this is the way Korean representatives should treat the representatives of China. This has to be communicated to the Korean Foreign Office, then to be handed over to the King, who must order his representatives to act accordingly." But notwithstanding the above command the King did not "order his representatives to act accordingly." His Majesty replied substantially that, while his Ministers would be instructed to show due respect and deference to the Ministers of China, yet as he had appointed in pursuance of all treaties with Korea full Ministers, he could not now change their titles without giving cause for unfavorable comment as well as unjust suspicions. Having therefore [been] appointed full Ministers they should, in their presentation at court, be governed by the rules of etiquette which govern the presentation of the Ministers from other countries; accordingly the original instructions to the Ministers, which do not contain any of the above conditions, were permitted to stand.

In this connection I take the liberty of quoting the following from an able letter written by a fearless and impartial correspondent on the independence of Korea some months ago. "The present action of China in this instance is an attempt to crush out the liberty of Korea, and comes within the scope of Art. 1st of the United States Treaty, which provides that if other powers (including of course China) deal unjustly or oppressively with Korea, America will use its good offices in her behalf. What Great Britain would do in the similar case of an envoy being appointed by the King of Korea to the Court of St. James being stopped by China from going there, may be safely inferred by its treaty stipulations with Korea, which in Art. 2nd provide that Korea as a high contracting party (no mention being made of the high suzerainty of China or of Korea being a vassal state) may appoint *a diplomatic representative to reside permanently in England with all the privileges and immunities that are enjoyed by the diplomatic functionaries in other countries.*

"Great Britain could not legally refuse to receive an envoy from Korea under her treaty. France, Germany, Italy and Russia have no doubt similar clauses in their treaties with Korea, and it remains to be seen how they will suffer and resent such preposterous interference on the part of China with Korea's right of Embassy after those powers have recognised it, should China presume to claim any pretext for limiting such right when Korean envoys are appointed to them.

"To all lovers of liberty and of principles in consonance with this grand mainspring of national life, it is surprising how this question of Korean liberty is treated by the British Press in China and Japan. Compare it with the excitement and declamations over the liberties of Bulgaria with its two millions of inhabitants and Roumelia with hardly one million of inhabitants, both composed of a motley mixture of semi-savage peoples. And yet Korea has twelve millions of people, all of the same race and civilized at least to an equal level with China and, forsooth, Korea is to be swallowed up by China and to be allowed to disappear from among the Eastern nations amidst the criminal silence and indifference of the humanitarian powers who are grief-stricken at even the possibility of the same happening in the corner of Eastern Europe. Does the effort of Korea to assert her liberty find favor with the British Press in China? Is there one clear, outspoken word to show that the public organs in the East are on the side of Korea in her struggle with China[?]"

As a matter of fact the Korean Minister to Washington was promptly and without any question presented to the President by the Honorable Secretary of State, and to the Secretary of State independently of the Chinese Minister, notwithstanding the many careless and untruthful assertions to the contrary, and just as the Minister to the European courts will be presented upon his arrival. If the Chinese Ministers in Europe were to attempt the anomalous proceeding of presenting the Korean Minister to those Courts it would not be carried out, for there is no country of respectability, jealous of its national honor, that will care to attempt to set the absurd and unprecedented example of receiving a plenipotentiary, envoy or minister of any sort from a vassal state. Even the so-called memorial (letter) which the King addressed to the Emperor of China, in answer to questions from Peking, explaining his reasons for as well as his right to send Ministers to Europe and America, is regarded by China and by vassalage advocates as another link in the chain by which they hope to bind Korea irretrievably to the Celestial Empire.

The trouble seems to arise from this: the language used by the King to express his *tributary* relations, is persistently and erroneously interpreted to mean *vassal* relations by China and her supporters. When the King refers, in the so-called memorial to the Emperor, to tributary envoys and plenipotentiaries, he is entirely consistent with international jurisprudence as interpreted and followed by other nations in their intercourse with each other, while China's appellation of vassal envoys and plenipotentiaries is a misnomer because entirely inconsistent with the laws of civilised nations. Such laws do not recognise vassal envoys, plenipotentiaries or ministers of any kind, for the reason that vassal states have the power to create only consuls and commercial agents. In this connection there is another device which deserves attention, and that is this: letters or documents, written or translated to suit the occasion, are frequently published by the press in China, purporting to be from the King of Korea, inferentially if not positively admitting Korea's vassalage. In answer to such statements I am informed upon the very best authority that the King has never admitted in documents or otherwise the existence of such relations, and further, *if anything has been admitted by any official of the Government at any time which even implies vassalage, it is without authority and void*. The King knows only too well the object of the insidious conduct of China towards his country; aside from this, he cannot be induced or intimidated into admitting a national fallacy. Even if dependent relations could be created by admissions, and the King, under the threatening, violent and criminal treatment of China for two and a-half years past, were to admit vassalage in the most abject way, it should not be binding upon his Government, for admissions under duress are not only no evidence of a fact but they are no admissions. Other independent states, with but few commercial interests to protect and no questions of sovereignty to settle, dispatch to foreign countries public ministers and nothing is said against it, but when the King of Korea, in accordance with the expressed stipulations in all the treaties with other independent powers, does the same thing, a perfect shower of invective greets the public ear from some quarters while from others, more mild, the act is characterised as mischievous and ill-advised; that it was forcing to the front a question which ought to have been kept in the background while the King and his advisors turned their attention to the development of the resources of the country.

It is quite true that the question was forced to the front, not by the King and his advisors but by the tyranny and oppression of China, largely through the conduct of Commissioner Yuan, which, for petty schemes, criminality, injustice and brutality has seldom, if ever, been equalled in the annals of international intercourse. With a view to placing the heel of China on the neck of Korea, he has not only opposed almost every effort which has been made in the direction of internal development but he has, through the mercenary brigade which he always keeps about him, attempted to bring failure and ridicule upon almost every effort the better class of Koreans have made to transact business for the government or themselves, in order to make it appear that the Koreans are but a nation of helpless children who can never learn business and who, for that reason, need a Chinese guardian over them. He has threatened the King repeatedly through certain Korean officials with the Chinese army and navy and with the vengeance of the Viceroy, in order to compel compliance with his wishes and demands, while to weaken the royal authority in the eyes of officials and subjects alike he has abused and trampled upon the long-established and sacred customs of the court by riding in his chair into the Palace almost up to the very entrance leading to the presence of the King, accompanied by his coolies, servants and horsemen, who at times have conducted themselves in a disorderly manner; while in the excitement of July and August of 1886, which he was the principal cause of, arising out of his attempt to force the government to admit that the King was the author of a letter his Majesty never wrote, and which was said to contain a request for the protection of a friendly power against the aggressions of China, the language and conduct of China's representative would have done credit to the chief of braggadocios. In some of his conduct he has been more or less applauded and encouraged by one or two foreign officials, while in all of his disreputable work he has been much assisted by a few petty Chinese officials as well as by certain of China's gun-boats sent to the open ports in Korea for the purpose of "protecting Chinese consuls and merchants" as stipulated in their treaty, and as alleged and published in the preamble to such treaty *"as a favor granted by China to a dependent state,"* which have been detected in some of their attempts to smuggle red ginseng out of the country. These gun-boats also on their arrival from China are in the habit of bringing more or less cargo which their officers demand shall be landed without examination, while the Customs' authorities urge the right of inspection as in ordinary cases to see whether or not it contains dutiable goods. Invariably when disputes of this character arise the Chinese Consul takes up the side of the gun-boat people and in their behalf appeals to Commissioner Yuan in Seoul, who in turn threatens the President of the Foreign Office until the order is given to pass the goods without examination. The last case of smuggling ginseng by one of these gun-boats, so far as is known, occurred in October, when several thousand dollars worth of the drug were seized, the largest chest of which, *was covered by the seal and signature of Commissioner Yuan*. The Chief Commissioner of Customs [Henry F. Merrill] has done all in his power to break up these lawless and fraudulent practices. He has appealed to the President of the Foreign Office, to the Viceroy at Tientsin and to the Inspector-General of Customs in China to aid him in enforcing the laws and regulations of the Korean Customs service, but thus far without avail. The President of the Foreign Office frankly says he is powerless as against the Chinese in these matters. Even with the fraudulent treatment it has received, the Customs revenues for the year just closed amounted to the sum of $250,000.00, a sum which, under legitimate and fair treatment, would have been considerably increased.

But the culminating act of China's representative, for cold-blooded wickedness, lays in his plot, exposed in July last, to dethrone and carry off the King to make temporary room for a pliant tool. The execution of this diabolical business involved riot, arson, bloodshed and probable assassinations, besides imperiling the lives of all the foreigners in Seoul as well as those of many native people. Every detail of this conspiracy is in possession of the King, and which would no doubt have been carried out but for the integrity and loyalty of Prince Min Yong Ik, one of the ablest and truest of Korean subjects, who, with the knowledge of the King, had been let into the plot, and who faithfully reported its different phases from time to time to His Majesty as well as myself, enabling us thereby to control and defeat it. Perhaps the most extraordinary part of this infamous business is the draft of it, which was to have been submitted to the Viceroy for approval or rejection.

The principal features of this draft were as follows:—Native soldiers were to be drilled at Kang Wha under the pretext of garrisoning the point against the "outside barbarians." These soldiers were to be reviewed by the Chinese representative in order that they might readily recognise their commander at the critical moment. They were to be placed conveniently near to the palace. Then the Tai Wan Kiun [Taewŏn'gun] or ex-regent's palace or house was to be fired and the work of the incendiary laid at the door of the King, which was to be the signal for an uprising of the ex-regent's following, who hate the queen and her party with intense bitterness. The rioters were to attack the palace, when Commissioner Yuan was to appear on the ground, as he did in 1884, and in command of the troops already referred to, under the pretence of quelling the rioters, was to take possession of the person of the King and carry him out of the palace, and then declare the son of the King's elder brother heir-apparent and the ex-regent regent, until the heir agreed upon attained his majority, thereby enabling the Chinese, under the direction of the regent, to thoroughly invest the government and country. Neither did China's representative neglect the financial part of the scheme, for he placed in the hands of a certain General 3,000 Taels (about $4,500.00) out of which the expenses of drilling and moving the troops were to be paid. This sum was however returned to the Chinese Legation after the departure of Min Yong Ik and the collapse of the conspiracy.

The Chinese Government cannot plead ignorance of the conduct of their officials in Korea, for they have been fully advised from time to time through different channels. Twice I visited Tientsin under authority from the King, when the fullest discussions were had with the Viceroy with respect to the extraordinary conduct of the Chinese representative and the policy of the Pekin Government towards Korea. In my first interview, in September 1886, I urged an amicable understanding between China and Russia as well as Japan, in regard to the political affairs of the peninsula, as the surest means of preventing irritation and disorder, and before my return the Viceroy assured me that such an understanding would not only be reached but that China would change her representative, as Yuan was too young not only in years but also in experience for such a post; in fact, said the Viceroy, the position has already been tendered to the present Taotai of Tientsin and the Taotai who has just been appointed at Chefoo, but that both had declined. On the occasion of my second visit, in October of last year, to discuss Korea's right to send public ministers abroad and to open ports in the interest of trade, as well as to protest against Yuan's latest conspiracy against the King, if it became necessary, in one interview, finding that the Viceroy turned a deaf ear to everything reflecting in any way upon that official, I was about to dispose of him once [and] for all, as I supposed, by presenting the indisputable evidences of his recent treasonable conduct, when, to my amazement, the Viceroy coolly informed me that he knew all about the dethronement scheme; that while Yuan was in it, yet it was all the fault of Min Yong Ik, who laid the plot and induced Yuan to go into it, and that for his stupidity in letting himself be drawn into such a thing he had been severely reprimanded. And still, in the face of this criminal record, Yuan continues the representative of China to Korea, in violation of the closing paragraph of the first article of the treaty between the two countries, which says:—"Should any such officer disclose waywardness, masterfulness or improper conduct of public business, the Superintendent of Trade for the Northern Port and the King of Korea respectively will notify each other of the fact *and at once recall him*."

In view of all this the inquiry naturally suggests itself, why is the Commissioner kept in Seoul? Is it because China, desiring to take possession of Korea and having no excuse in the eyes of civilized nations for doing so, expects him, through his violent conduct, to furnish one? It is to be hoped not. Nor is this all; what must be the moral status of a government which insists on being represented at the court of a neighboring state by a smuggler, conspirator and diplomatic outlaw? I submit the language is not too strong, in view of the facts and the following historical record applicable to them, copied from a well-known author on international law:—"Several instances are to be found in history of Ambassadors being seized and sent out of the country. The Bishop of Ross, Ambassador of Mary Queen of Scots, was imprisoned and then banished from England for conspiring against the Sovereign, while the Duke of Norfolk and other conspirators were *tried and executed*. In 1584 De Mendoza, the Spanish Ambassador in England, was ordered to quit the realm for conspiring to introduce troops to dethrone Queen Elizabeth. In 1684 De Bass, the French Minister, was ordered to depart the country in 24 hours, on a charge of conspiring against the life of Cromwell. In 1717 Gyllenborg, the Swedish Ambassador, contrived a plot to dethrone George I. He was arrested, his cabinet broken open and searched and his papers seized. Sweden arrested the British Minister at Stockholm by way of reprisal. The arrest of Gyllenborg was necessary as a measure of self-defence, but on no principle of international law can the arrest of the British Minister by Sweden be made justifiable. For similar reasons, Callamare, Spanish Ambassador in France, was in 1718 arrested, his papers seized and himself conducted to the frontier by military escort. So recently as 1848 Sir H. Bulwer, the British Ambassador in Spain, had his passports returned, and was requested to leave Spanish territory by the government. Certain disturbances had taken place in certain parts of Spain, and the Government persuaded themselves that Sir H. Bulwer had lent his assistance to the disaffection." And had the Korean Government possessed the national strength to enforce their rights, another case of far more recent date would have been added to the above list in the person of Commissioner Yuan. The Chinese authorities seemed to be considerably exercised over the surrender of Kim Ok Kiun [Kim Ok-kyun] by the Japanese Government, in order that he might be justly punished for his conspiracy, and who would doubtless have been willingly given up by that government were not international precedents against the surrender of political offenders; and yet the conspiracies of the Chinese representative are of a far graver character than those of Kim Ok Kiun, for the former's were directed against the King, the head and front of all government in the kingdom, while the latter's were directed more against certain high officials than otherwise.

If the Chinese authorities were sincere in their efforts to have Kim Ok

Kiun properly punished for his crimes, then they surely will not condone the greater offence of their own representative against the King now. The oppressive conduct of China is not confined alone to her small officials in Korea, not to those who periodically visit the country in gun-boats, for it extends to Tientsin and Pekin.

After my return from the northern part of Korea, where I went to inspect the natural resources of the country, I recommended among other things that as Ping Yang [P'yŏngyang] is the centre of a large section of country, rich in agricultural and mineral wealth, legitimate trade would be encouraged and increased, the Customs' revenues largely augmented, the smuggling carried on in and out of the Tatong [Taedong] river checked, while the preliminary work of opening the valuable coal and other mines located near there—already determined upon by the government—would be facilitated by establishing an open port at or near that city. The proposition was also warmly supported by the Chief Commissioner of Customs, and subsequently that efficient officer was instructed by the King to take the preliminary steps. A steamer was dispatched with a Customs' officer on board to survey the river and to locate the port at the nearest practical point to Ping Yang. While this work was going on the Chief Commissioner was informed by China's representative that the Viceroy Li would not permit a port to be opened at that place. The Chief Commissioner, humiliated by this unjust and unwarrantable interference, was compelled to direct the vessel with the Customs' officer to return. At first the King declined to believe that such an order could emanate from the Viceroy, but direct communication with the Chung Tang through myself confirmed the statement of China's representative. In the discussion of this subject the Viceroy based his objection upon the erroneous and illogical grounds that, as Ping Yang is near the port of Newchwang in China, an open port there would seriously interfere with Chinese trade. In the first place, Newchwang is several hundred miles from Ping Yang, and secondly, there is not annually a thousand dollars worth of trade carried on between the two points. But if there were even one million dollars worth or ten for that matter, are the revenues of the Korean Government entitled to no consideration by China? Or was it the object of the Pekin Government in getting control of the Customs service of Korea to so direct and manipulate it as to make the natural resources and wealth of the country subserve the interests of China instead of Korea? The right of every state to increase its wealth, population and power by opening ports for the stimulation and encouragement of trade, the extension of its navigation, the improvement of its revenues, arts, agriculture and commerce, is incontrovertible and is recognized by every civilized nation under the sun, and the sooner China is compelled to recognize the fact also, the better it will be for the family of nations whose comity and friendship she essays to share, as well as for her own interests. Neither do the commands of the Viceroy stop at opening ports, for His Excellency asserts that Korea cannot negotiate loans with which to aid in the development of the natural resources of the country, or transact in her own way, as she has for centuries past, the business of the government, without first asking and obtaining the consent of China. In view of such a long train of cruel, unjust and tyrannical conduct as is here presented, China's professions of friendship for Korea, under the claim of suzerainty, become simply monstrous in their sincerity.

Nor do the mischievous consequences of such meddlesomeness stop here; for if the Viceroy in his commands to the Korean Government can practically defeat the commercial part of the treaties made with other countries, His Excellency can, by similar commands, nullify every stipulation of those agreements, whether they apply to the appointment of public ministers, opening ports for the convenience of trade, the collection of duties, or to the rights of citizens and subjects of the treaty powers, whether of person or property. How long the treaty rights of other countries and the lives of their nationals are to be jeopardized and trifled with, or how far China will be permitted to go in the direction she now seems to be heading before a halt is called, depends entirely upon the faith and value other powers besides the United States attach to their stipulations with Korea. I say other powers besides the United States because that government, with no political interests in the peninsula to protect has, through their distinguished Secretary of State, having in mind the faith pledged in the first article of the American treaty, informed China that, as the former has concluded a treaty of friendship and commerce with Korea on the basis of a sovereign and independent state, they expect the rights and privileges so acquired to be respected. Were the national autonomy of China endangered or the rights and immunities of her subjects threatened with destruction by the continued independence of Korea, and China were for that reason to proceed openly to annex the country instead of assuming relations with it which do not exist and endeavoring by false pretenses to sustain the assumption, the case would be different. For the right of self-preservation is just as inherent in a nation as it is in individuals, while the most solemn and responsible obligation it owes to its people is the guarantee of all their rights under a stable and well-administered government.

The King having appointed and dispatched public ministers to all countries in treaty relations with Korea,—a course so fatal to the claim of vassalage,—the time has surely come for China to quit masquerading with the Korean question and frankly announce in unmistakeable terms her policy toward the peninsula; for until the question is settled one way or the other, it will not only continue as now to be a very serious and disturbing element in the politics of the East but it will delay, if not prevent, internal development and the reformation of long-established abuses in Korea. But with the question settled in favor of the continued independence of the country, and entire responsibility for the duties and obligations already assumed through the government's international agreements, and with labor made honorable by royal decree and idleness condemned as it is in Western countries, where the fact is recognised that the only key to real greatness, permanent prosperity and national strength, lies in the recognition of the truth that, to engage in all branches of labor and business enterprises is not only respectable but it is more, it is laudable and worthy of the highest commendation and encouragement. Then with the idle Yang Ban class (so-called gentlemen), which are now feeding upon and exhausting the labor of the country because it is considered dishonorable for them to do any work, compelled to earn the bread they eat, and the agricultural classes stimulated and encouraged by the protection of their surplus products from the squeezing and other illegal exactions now made upon it—sure to follow sooner or later under settled political conditions—Korea would then enter upon that era of prosperity which the natural wealth of the country so justly merits.

A few words now in reply to the stale charge that the King is weak and vacillating in character and I leave the subject of Korea's sovereignty and grievances to those who are better able to protect and right them. And upon this point, two years' experience as His Majesty's Foreign Advisor and Vice-President of the Home Office (Privy Council) should enable me to speak advisedly; for during that time some of the most trying phases of the Korean problem have presented themselves for solution, and through them all the King has shown a firmness, cheerfulness and patience worthy of a ruler of a great nation. Often his language and bearing have indicated great anxiety but never weakness or anger. It is true that, since Korea's contact with Western people, dazzled by the glitter and novelty of the change and encouraged by the smooth words of some adventurers and some unscrupulous persons, the government have been led into under-taking impracticable ventures whose failures have created a reputation for extravagance and fickleness which will perhaps take years of prudence and economy to remove; but every Asiatic nation has had to pass through such an experience and Korea must have hers also. After dispatching the ministers to Europe and America against the Imperial protests of China, the King ought not to be longer accused of either fear or a want of firmness of character. His Majesty received the protest with that quiet dignity which had characterised his bearing in other important matters and after hearing and carefully weighing China's objections—relying on his right as expressed in and guaranteed by the treaties, as well as by the law of nations—the ministers were ordered to leave for their respective posts, against the ultimatum of the Pekin Government and the positive conditions prescribed by the Viceroy, as well as in the face of the blustering conduct and diplomatic antics of Commissioner Yuan, supplemented by the persistent efforts of a few cowardly Korean officials, whose well-beaten track between the palace and the Chinese Legation indicates the character of their patriotism as well as their devotion to their King. No, from my own knowledge I should rather say that His Majesty is far too strong in character to suit those whose purposes it serves not to have it so. It must be borne in mind also that His Majesty has no kingdom to gain through an arrogant exhibition of *strength*, but he has one to lose through an exhibition of weakness or fear. The King's character for universal kindness may have been mistaken for weakness. Even some of his subjects say His Majesty is too kind for the good of the public service. His habits are those of perfect sobriety and industry, and being progressive in his nature, he is constantly seeking information which will aid him in directing his subjects into those paths that lead to the higher plains of civilization which have done so much to humanize and Christianize the Western World. Unfortunately in this great work the King, with a few exceptions, stands alone. Those who are in sympathy with Western progress are, as a rule, without influence or following, while those who possess both adhere to the traditions of the past with a loyalty worthy of better things. Under these circumstances the King of Korea surely deserves the sympathy and support of all good people.

Seoul, Korea,   O. N. DENNY
 February 3rd, 1888.

Notes

Editor's Introduction

1. For examples of some of the studies dealing with this period see Ch'oe Yŏng-hŭi [Choe Young Hee] et al., eds., *Han'guksa* [History of Korea], 24 vols. (Seoul: Kuksa p'yŏnch'an wiwŏnhoe, 1975–78), especially vols. 16–17; Sin Kuk-chu, *Han'guk kŭndae chŏngch'i oegyosa* [A history of modern Korean politics and diplomacy] (Seoul: T'amgudang, 1968); Yi Kwang-nin [Lee Kwang-rin], *Han'guk kaehwasa yŏn'gu* [A study of the history of enlightenment in Korea] (Seoul: Ilchogak, 1969); Hilary Conroy, *The Japanese Seizure of Korea, 1868–1910: A Study of Realism and Idealism in International Relations* (Philadelphia: University of Pennsylvania Press, 1974); C. I. Eugene Kim and Han-kyo Kim, *Korea and the Politics of Imperialism, 1876–1910* (Berkeley and Los Angeles: University of California Press, 1967); James B. Palais, *Politics and Policy in Traditional Korea* (Cambridge: Harvard University Press, 1975).

2. Kim Wŏn-mo, *Kŭndae Han-Mi kyosŏpsa* [A modern history of Korean-American relations] (Seoul: Hongsŏngsa, 1979), pp. 173–91, 217–371; Ching Young Choe, *The Rule of the Taewŏn'gun, 1864–1873: Restoration in Yi Korea* (Cambridge: East Asian Research Center, Harvard University, 1972), pp. 91–133.

3. Martina Deuchler, *Confucian Gentlemen and Barbarian Envoys: The Opening of Korea, 1875–1885* (Seattle: University of Washington Press, 1977), pp. 11–50.

4. Chŏng Yong-sŏk, *Miguk ŭi taeHan chŏngch'aek, 1845–1980* [The two Korean policies of the United States, 1845–1980] (Seoul: Ilchogak, 1979), pp. 7–39.

5. On the Korean-American treaty see Deuchler, *Confucian Gentlemen and Barbarian Envoys*, pp. 110–22; Charles O. Paullin, *Diplomatic Negotiations of American Naval Officers, 1778–1883* (Baltimore: The Johns Hopkins Press, 1912; reprint ed., Gloucester, Mass.: Peter Smith, 1967), pp. 294–328; Han U-gŭn [Han Woo-keun], "Shufeldt chedok ŭi Han-Mi suho choyak kyosŏp ch'ujin yŏnyu e taehayŏ" [A study on the reasons for sending Commodore Shufeldt to open negotiations with Korea in 1880], *Chindan hakpo* 24 (August 1963):7–22; Yi Po-hyŏng, "Shufeldt

chedok kwa 1880nyŏn ŭi Cho-Mi kyosŏp" [Commodore Shufeldt and the attempt to open Korea in 1880], *Yŏksa hakpo* 15 (September 1961):61–91. For copies of the treaty itself in both Chinese and English, see *KuHanmal choyak hwich'an* [Treaties of the late Yi dynasty] (Seoul: Kukhoe tosŏgwan, 1965), 26:294–305.

6. See Yur-Bok Lee, *Diplomatic Relations Between the United States and Korea, 1866–1887* (New York: Humanities Press, 1970), pp. 52–186; Donald M. Bishop, "Policy and Personality in Early Korean-American Relations: The Case of George Clayton Foulk," in *The United States and Korea: American-Korean Relations, 1866–1976,* ed. Andrew C. Nahm (Kalamazoo: The Center for Korean Studies, Western Michigan University, 1979), pp. 27–63.

7. Mun Il-p'yŏng, *Han-Mi osipnyŏnsa* [A fifty-year history of Korean-American relations], ed. Yi Kwang-nin (Seoul: Chogwangsa, 1945; reprint ed., Seoul: T'amgudang, 1975); Pak Il-gŭn, *Kŭndae Han-Mi oegyosa* [A history of modern Korean-American diplomatic relations] (Seoul: Pakusa, 1968); Fred Harvey Harrington, *God, Mammon, and the Japanese: Dr. Horace N. Allen and Korean-American Relations, 1884–1905* (Madison: University of Wisconsin Press, 1944); Jeffery M. Dorwart, "The Independent Minister: John M. B. Sill and the Struggle against Japanese Expansion in Korea, 1894–1897," *Pacific Historical Review* 44 (November 1975):485–505; Robert R. Swartout, Jr., "United States Ministers to Korea, 1882–1905: The Loss of American Innocence," *Transactions of the Royal Asiatic Society, Korea Branch* 57 (1982):29–40.

8. See Harrington, *God, Mammon, and the Japanese;* Spencer J. Palmer, *Korea and Christianity: The Problem of Identification with Tradition* (Seoul: Hollym Corporation, Publishers, 1967).

9. In employing Western advisers Korea was following in the footsteps of both China and Japan. For a study of this process see Jonathan Spence, *To Change China: Western Advisers in China, 1620–1960* (Boston: Little, Brown & Co., 1969). Many of the documents pertaining to Korea's employment of such advisers are contained in George M. McCune and John A. Harrison, eds., *Korean-American Relations: Documents Pertaining to the Far Eastern Diplomacy of the United States, Vol. I: The Initial Period, 1883–1886* (Berkeley and Los Angeles: University of California Press, 1951), pp. 53–65; Spencer J. Palmer, ed., *Korean-American Relations: Documents Pertaining to the Far Eastern Diplomacy of the United States, Vol. II: The Period of Growing Influence, 1887–1895* (Berkeley and Los Angeles: University of California Press, 1963), pp. 141–83.

10. Deuchler, *Confucian Gentlemen and Barbarian Envoys,* pp. 86–92, 114–22; Frederick Foo Chien, *The Opening of Korea: A Study of*

Chinese Diplomacy, 1876–1885 (Hamden, Conn.: The Shoe String Press, 1967), pp. 60–93; Key-Hiuk Kim, *The Last Phase of the East Asian World Order: Korea, Japan, and the Chinese Empire, 1860–1882* (Berkeley and Los Angeles: University of California Press, 1980), pp. 273–316.

11. Kwŏn Sŏk-pong, "Imo gunbyŏn" [The 1882 military riot], in Ch'oe Yŏng-hŭi et al., eds., *Han'guksa*, 16:392–441; Yu Hong-nyŏl, "Kapsin chŏngbyŏn" [The 1884 political coup], in ibid., pp. 500–50; Deuchler, *Confucian Gentlemen and Barbarian Envoys*, pp. 131–34, 205–12; Key-Hiuk Kim, *The Last Phase of the East Asian World Order*, pp. 316–27.

12. Mrs. Owen N. Denny, "Facts in the Biography of Judge Denny," unpublished manuscript, Owen N. Denny Papers, Private Collection of William C. Ralston, Portland, Oregon, p. 12. In her manuscript Mrs. Denny wrote that "the Judge was loath to go [to Korea], for he had made preparations to remain in America. His friends, however, advised him to accept this opportunity, he was still young, and he could return later and still find his place awaiting him."

13. Robert R. Swartout, Jr., *Mandarins, Gunboats, and Power Politics: Owen Nickerson Denny and the International Rivalries in Korea* (Honolulu: The University Press of Hawaii, 1980), pp. 1–2. This is the only detailed study of Denny's diplomatic career.

14. Ibid.

15. Virginia C. Holmgren, *Chinese Pheasants, Oregon Pioneers* (Portland: Oregon Historical Society, 1964), p. 9. As the title of Holmgren's study implies, Denny was involved with pheasants. In fact, while U.S. consul general in Shanghai, Denny arranged for the shipment of numerous Chinese pheasants to the United States. Because of Denny's dedicated efforts the beautiful birds are now found throughout much of North America.

16. The original Tientsin commission is located in the Denny Papers, Ralston Collection.

17. Mrs. Denny, "Facts in the Biography of Judge Denny," pp. 2–3.

18. The Chinese term for self-strengthening was *tzu-ch'iang*. For a historiographical analysis of this important movement see Thomas L. Kennedy, "Self-Strengthening: An Analysis Based on Some Recent Writings," *Ch'ing-shih wen-t'i* 3 (November 1974):3–35. For an example of Li Hung-chang's interest in industrial development see Thomas L. Kennedy, *The Arms of Kiangnan: Modernization in the Chinese Ordinance Industry, 1860–1895* (Boulder, Col.: Westview Press, 1978), pp. 34–77.

19. Li to Grant, May 26, 1881, Denny Papers, Ralston Collection.

20. On the Denny-Seward controversy see Swartout, *Mandarins, Gunboats, and Power Politics*, pp. 10–16.

21. Denny to Adee, October 9, 1883, No. 455, United States, Department of State, Despatches from United States Consuls in Shanghai, 1847–1906 (File Microcopies of Records in the National Archives, Washington, D.C.: No. 112), Roll 35.

22. I have borrowed Professor Young I. Lew's estimate of $15,360. See Young I. Lew, "American Advisers in Korea, 1885–1894: Anatomy of Failure," in Nahm, ed., *The United States and Korea*, p. 70.

23. Note the illustrations of the Denny residence in the present volume.

24. For Denny's role in the negotiations and signing of the Franco-Korean treaty see Swartout, *Mandarins, Gunboats, and Power Politics*, pp. 60–65. This book also contains an English translation of the treaty (pp. 153–59). For French and Chinese versions of the treaty see *KuHanmal choyak hwich'an*, 27:96–112.

25. For Denny's role in the Russo-Korean agreement see Swartout, *Mandarins, Gunboats, and Power Politics*, pp. 129–32. For copies of the agreement in English and Korean see *KuHanmal choyak hwich'an*, 27:65–80.

26. Yi Yong-hŭi, "Kŏmundo chŏmryŏng oegyo chonggo" [Diplomacy respecting the occupation of Kŏmundo], in *Yi Sang-baek Paksa hoegap ki'nyŏmnon ch'ong* [Essay collection in commemoration of the sixtieth birthday of Dr. Yi Sang-baek] (Seoul: Ŭryu munhwasa, 1964), pp. 459–99; Yung Chung Kim, "Great Britain and Korea, 1883–1887" (Ph.D. dissertation, Indiana University, 1965), chs. 4–5.

27. For example, see Denny to Li, June 29, 1886, Letter 15 herein.

28. Watters to Kim, March 1, 1887, in Koryŏ taehakkyo Asea munje yŏn'guso, ed., *KuHan'guk oegyo munsŏ* [Documents relating to the foreign relations of old Korea], 22 vols. (Seoul, Koryŏ taehakkyo ch'ulp'ansa, 1965–73), *Yŏngan* [documents with Great Britain], 13: 223–24.

29. O. N. Denny, *China and Korea* (Shanghai: Kelly & Walsh, 1888), pp. 25–27; Denby to Bayard, December 9, 1887, No. 521, with enclosure, in Palmer, ed., *Korean-American Relations*, pp. 109–12.

30. On Pak's mission to the United States see Swartout, *Mandarins, Gunboats, and Power Politics*, pp. 89–95; Yur-Bok Lee, "Korean Relations with the United States, 1887–1889: A Study of Conflict Between Old Confucian World Order and Modern International Relations," a paper presented at the 32nd Annual Meeting of the Association for Asian Studies, Washington, D.C., March 21–23, 1980.

31. For Denny's feud with Yuan Shih-k'ai see Swartout, *Mandarins, Gunboats, and Power Politics*, chs. 4–5. For studies on Yuan, see Jerome

Ch'en, *Yuan Shih-k'ai*, 2nd ed. (Stanford: Stanford University Press, 1972); Lin Ming-te, *Yüan Shih-k'ai yü Ch'ao-hsien* [Yuan Shih-k'ai and Korea] (Nan-Kang: Chung yang yen chiu yüan chin tai shih yen chiu so, 1970).

32. See Appendix B.

33. For an analysis of Denny's economic views of Korea see Swartout, *Mandarins, Gunboats, and Power Politics*, ch. 6.

34. For example, see Denny to General [Kennedy], July 21, 1889, Letter 10; Denny to Han, October 6, 1889, Letter 11.

35. Hosea B. Morse, *The International Relations of the Chinese Empire*, 3 vols. (London: Longmans, Green, and Co., 1918), 3:18.

36. Swartout, *Mandarins, Gunboats, and Power Politics*, pp. 120–21.

37. The Chinese even put pressure on the U.S. government in an attempt to block American loans to Korea. See Tsui to Blaine, May 6, 1890, in Palmer, ed., *Korean-American Relations*, p. 19.

38. Denny himself had a very low opinion of the traditional *yangban* elite. In his booklet, *China and Korea*, he described this group as a class that was "feeding upon and exhausting the labor of the country because it is considered dishonorable for them to do any work." See Appendix B.

39. Yur-Bok Lee, *Diplomatic Relations Between the United States and Korea, 1866–1887*, pp. 163–86.

40. Swartout, *Mandarins, Gunboats, and Power Politics*, pp. 103–06.

41. On the other hand, we should recognize that the publication of *China and Korea* did help to "clear away some of the cobwebs" (as Denny put it) regarding Chinese claims of suzerainty over Korea. By the late 1880s Sino-Korean relations, like all international relationships in Northeast Asia, had moved away from the old Confucian patterns. The nations of the region, regardless of whether or not Chinese officials wanted to publicly admit it, had entered a new phase of international relations based largely upon Western practice and law. See Key-Hiuk Kim, *The Last Phase of the East Asian World Order*, pp. 4–15, 328–51; Swartout, *Mandarins, Gunboats, and Power Politics*, pp. 31, 37–44, 106–21.

42. Denny to Wetmore, June 20, 1886, Letter 2.

43. Denny finally left Korea in January 1891 after collecting his back pay and arrived at his home in Portland in July of the same year. In the decade before his death in 1900 he remained in his home state, serving as a receiver at the Portland Savings Bank and as a state senator from 1892 to 1896. Despite the frustrations he felt during his last months in Korea, Denny and his wife retained many warm sentiments for the peninsular kingdom. They took pride in showing guests their mementos from Seoul, especially those received from the royal family.

The Letters of Owen N. Denny

1. Before arriving in Korea in the spring of 1886, the Dennys stopped briefly in Yokohama, Japan. On February 8, 1886, their Yokohama hotel, the Windsor House, caught fire from an adjoining photograph gallery. Although the couple suffered no lasting injuries from the blaze, they did lose about $2,000 worth of personal property. This loss did much to create a financial hardship for the Dennys that was to plague them for the next four years.

2. For an accurate description of the Dennys' residence, see the various photographs herein.

3. For discussions of the 1886 Franco-Korean treaty, see Swartout, *Mandarins, Gunboats, and Power Politics*, pp. 60–65; Ch'oe Sŏk-u, "Han-Pul choyak kwa sin'gyo chayu" [The Korean-French treaty and religious freedom], *Sahak yŏn'gu* 21 (September 1969): 209–29.

4. W.S. Wetmore was an American businessman in Shanghai, China, and a close personal friend of Owen Denny's. Their friendship dated back to Denny's days as U.S. consul general in that city.

5. Denny was referring to Paul Georg von Moellendorff, who had served as adviser to the Korean Foreign Office and head of the Korean Maritime Customs Service from 1882 to 1885. Von Moellendorff had been forced out of these positions by the Chinese because of his attempts to obtain Russian military instructors for Korea. Li Hung-chang's dissatisfaction with von Moellendorff's actions was one of the primary reasons for the Viceroy's efforts to bring Owen Denny to Seoul. Von Moellendorff and Denny thus became bitter rivals for the post of adviser to King Kojong. For an example of von Moellendorff's attitude toward Denny see his article, "A Reply to Mr. O. N. Denny's pamphlet entitled: 'China and Korea,'" in Rosalie von Moellendorff, *P. G. von Moellendorff, Ein Lebensbild* (Leipzig: Otto Harrassowitz, 1930), pp. 125–36. For studies of his life in Korea see Ko Pyŏng-ik, "Mok In-dŏk ŭi kobing kwa kŭ paegyŏng" [Von Moellendorff's employment and its background], *Chindan hakpo* 25–27 (December 1964):225–44; Deuchler, *Confucian Gentlemen and Barbarian Envoys*, pp. 158–64; Yur-Bok Lee, "Von Möllendorff and Big Power Intervention in Korea in the 1880s," a paper presented at the 29th Annual Meeting of the Midwest Conference on Asian Affairs, University of Iowa, October 24–25, 1980; Philip M. Woo, "The Historical Development of Korean Tariff and Customs Administration, 1875–1958" (Ph.D. dissertation, New York University, 1963), pp. 34–55.

6. R. M. Brown was an American businessman operating out of Shanghai.

7. Robert W. Shufeldt, who had retired from the U.S. Navy following his successful negotiation of the 1882 Korean-American treaty, visited Korea during the winter of 1886–87. Rumors circulated in Seoul at that time that he planned to become an adviser to King Kojong, but in fact he was never to be employed by the Korean government. See also Owen N. Denny to Robert W. Shufeldt, August 11 and 25, 1886, Box 17, Robert Wilson Shufeldt Papers, Library of Congress, Washington, D.C.

8. John W. Heron and Horace G. Underwood were two of the earliest American missionaries in Korea. Denny stayed at the Underwood residence during his first days in Seoul. For information on the two missionaries see Daniel L. Gifford, "John W. Heron, M.D.," *Korean Repository* 4 (December 1897):441–43; Lillias Underwood, *Underwood of Korea: Being an Intimate Record of the Life and Work of the Rev. H. G. Underwood* (New York: Fleming H. Revell Co., 1918).

9. This rather mild rebuff of Allen was an indication of future conflict between the two men. See Denny to Frazar, November 23, 1889, Letter 37 herein; Allen to Ellinwood, December 29, 1886, Letterbook 1; Allen to Ellinwood, October 25, 1887, Letterbook 2; Allen to Ellinwood, April 24, 1890, Letterbook 3, Horace N. Allen Papers, New York Public Library.

10. Van B. DeLashmutt was an influential Oregonian and close personal friend of Denny's. Among his various achievements he served both as mayor of Portland and as president of the Oregon National Bank of Portland. See H. W. Scott, *History of Portland, Oregon: With Illustrations and Biographical Sketches of Prominent Citizens and Pioneers* (Syracuse, N.Y.: A. Mason and Co. 1890), pp. 533–35.

11. Chou Fu was one of Li Hung-chang's closest associates, serving with the Viceroy from 1861 to 1901. Among his various positions were Tientsin customs taotai and Chihli provincial judge. Because of these locations, and because of his ties with Li, Chou Fu became a close acquaintance of Denny's during the latter's consular service in China.

12. As already indicated, these financial problems plagued Denny throughout his four years in Korea. See especially Denny to Han, October 6, 1889, Letter 11; Denny to Bevin, April 8, 1890, Letter 13; Denny to Detring, August 8, 1888, Letter 28.

13. Hugh H. Dinsmore was U.S. minister to Korea from 1887 to 1890. A strong supporter of Korean independence and modernization, he often worked closely with Denny. For valuable information on Dinsmore see Yur-Bok Lee, *Diplomatic Relations Between the United States and Korea, 1866–1887*, pp. 163–86.

14. John G. Lee was one of four Americans—along with William M. Dye, Edmund H. Cummins, and Ferdinand J. H. Nienstend—who

arrived in Korea in 1888 to serve as military advisers to the Korean army. Lee and Cummins were particularly unfit for such duty and had to be dismissed by the Korean government before the end of 1889. Concerning some of the trouble these two men caused see the many documents in Palmer, ed., *Korean-American Relations*, pp. 146–67. For scholarly studies of this subject see Yi Kwang-nin [Lee Kwang-rin], "Miguk kunsa kyogwan ŭi ch'obing kwa yŏnmugong'wŏn" [The employment of American military instructors and the training grounds], *Chindan hakpo* 23 (1965):7–36; Donald M. Bishop, "Sustaining Korean Independence: American Military Missions to Korea, 1882–1896" (M.A. thesis, Ohio State University, 1974), pp. 108–27.

15. Charles Chaillé-Long, secretary of the U.S. legation in Seoul from 1887 to 1889. For Chaillé-Long's own self-serving account of his stay in Korea see his *My Life in Four Continents*, 2 vols. (London: Hutchinson and Co., 1912), 2:338–86.

16. The "General" was John D. Kennedy, then U.S. consul general in Shanghai.

17. Here Denny was referring to his December 1888 meeting with Chinese officials in Shanghai, which is discussed in the Introduction to this volume. The Korean government's final payment of Denny's first two-year contract, combined with the Chinese unwillingness to remove Yuan Shih-k'ai from his post in Seoul, thus convinced Denny to continue his work in Korea.

18. Denny was one of the very few Westerners in Seoul at this time who supported the Korean position during the incident. For a "typical" Western view see Chaillé-Long, *My Life in Four Continents*, 2:364–66.

19. On Denny's opinion of Willard I. Pierce see also Denny to Lindsley, October 7, 1889, Letter 34. Cf. Harrington, *God, Mammon, and the Japanese*, pp. 140–41.

20. Han Kyu-sŏl was perhaps Denny's most important contact in the Korean government next to King Kojong. For basic biographical information see Yi Hong-jik, ed., *Kuksa taesajŏn* [Encyclopedia of Korean history] (Seoul: Paekmansa, 1975), p. 1769.

21. Taels 1,000 was the equivalent of about $1,280, which meant that Denny had been willing to accept a 22 percent decrease in his salary when he originally signed his second two-year contract.

22. This letter indicated that Denny, who was finally about to leave Korea, was turning more of his attention to personal matters in the United States.

23. Li Hung-chang was often referred to as Li Chung Tang, the latter two characters indicating his title of "Grand Secretary." This letter from Denny to Li deals with the British occupation of Kŏmundo.

24. Denny's "return" was from Tientsin, where he had visited Li in March 1886 to discuss Korean affairs before assuming his official position in Seoul.

25. Although this Russian document was unsigned, it was probably written by Karl Waeber, the Russian chargé d'affaires in Seoul. Waeber and Denny had been close friends since the 1870s, when they both served in Tientsin. This friendship would eventually help result in the 1888 Russo-Korean trade agreement. Both men were critical of the British occupation of Port Hamilton. For more information on Waeber and Russian activities in Korea see George A. Lensen, *Balance of Intrigue: International Rivalry in Korea and Manchuria, 1884–1899*, 2 vols. (Gainesville: University Presses of Florida, 1982).

26. Gustav Detring, from Germany, was a member of the Chinese Maritime Customs Service. From 1877 to 1904 he worked for the service in Tientsin, where he also became Li Hung-chang's most trusted foreign adviser. Because of Detring's friendship with Denny, it was through him that Li approached the Oregonian in 1885 about becoming an adviser to King Kojong.

27. Detring and Denny created their own code for communications in order to protect themselves from unnecessary Chinese—and other foreign—criticism. Unfortunately the code was not contained in Denny's Letterbook; fortunately the two men almost never used the code, at least not in their letters I have examined.

28. Henry F. Merrill was head of the Korean Maritime Customs Service from October 1885 to November 1889. An American, Merrill had been recommended for his post by Li Hung-chang and Robert Hart, who himself was head of the Chinese Maritime Customs Service. Because Hart was his immediate superior, Merrill generally followed Hart's contention that Korea should be controlled by China. Yet as a result of Yuan Shih-k'ai's numerous excesses in Seoul, Merrill occasionally departed from this policy and actually worked with Denny to limit the Chinese representative's influence. For studies of Merrill's career in Korea see Woo, "The Historical Development of Korean Tariff and Customs Administration," pp. 55–68; Ko Pyŏng-ik, "Chosŏn hae'gwan kwa Ch'ŏngguk hae'gwan kwa ŭi kwan'gye—Merrill kwa Hart rŭl chungsim ŭro" [The relationship between the Korean and the Chinese Customs Service: Merrill and Hart], *Tonga munhwa* 4 (October 1965):1–29; Lew, "American Advisers in Korea, 1885–1894: Anatomy of Failure," in Nahm, ed., *The United States and Korea*, pp. 70–73.

29. "Aca" was part of the Detring-Denny code; it may have stood for King Kojong.

30. Yuan Shih-k'ai claimed in August 1886 that Kojong requested St.

Petersburg to make Korea a Russian protectorate. Denny insisted that no such request was made, that Yuan had invented the story as an excuse for removing Kojong from the throne. Yuan's "plot" fell through, but not before he and Denny had become bitter enemies. See Swartout, *Mandarins, Gunboats, and Power Politics*, pp. 81–88.

31. Yuan Shih-k'ai.

32. See also Foulk to Bayard, September 8, 1886, No. 3; Foulk to Bayard, October 14, 1886, No. 13, in McCune and Harrison, eds., *Korean-American Relations*, pp. 149–56.

33. The Dennys had just returned from a trip to Tientsin, where Owen Denny had met with Li Hung-chang in an attempt to remove the British from Port Hamilton and also to restrict the power of Yuan Shih-k'ai in Korea. On this visit see also Denny to Frazar, November 14, 1886, Letter 20.

34. During the next two years Denny's views toward Li Hung-chang were to change as he became much more critical of the Viceroy's Korean policy. For example, see Denny to Mitchell, February 6, 1888, Letter 23; Denny to Detring, September 22, 1888, Letter 30; Denny to Editor, *Chinese Times*, October 12, 1888, Letter 31; Swartout, *Mandarins, Gunboats, and Power Politics*, ch. 5.

35. See also Denny to Directors of the Nippon Yusen Kaisha Steam Ship Company, January 4, 1887, Letter 21.

36. On these Russo-Korean trade regulations see Swartout, *Mandarins, Gunboats, and Power Politics*, pp. 129–32.

37. Everett Frazar, a New York City businessman, served as Korea's consul general in that city for fourteen years in the 1880s and 1890s. An early American student of Korean affairs, Frazar also recommended Denny as the King's foreign adviser to both the Korean and American governments. See Frazar to Kim, December 8, 1885, *KuHan'guk oegyo munsŏ: Mian*, 10:199; Frazar to Bayard, October 29, 1885, Thomas F. Bayard Papers, Library of Congress, Washington, D.C.; Everett Frazar, *Korea, and Her Relations to China, Japan, and the United States* (Orange, N.J.: Chronicle Book and Job Printing Office, 1884).

38. John Lindsley was Everett Frazar's business representative in Yokohama, Japan, and as such became deeply involved in Denny's plans for Korean economic development. See many of the letters contained in Section IV of this volume.

39. See note 3, above.

40. Lo Feng-lu, the highest graduate of China's Foochow Arsenal School in 1871, served for many years as Li Hung-chang's confidential secretary.

41. For a copy of this "memoranda," which in many ways was an early

draft of Denny's *China and Korea* booklet, see Denny to Dinsmore, November 8, 1887, containing "A Memoranda submitted to His Excellency Li Chung Tang at Tientsin on Oct. 7th 1887 on Corean Affairs by Mr. Denny the King's Advisor, and discussion thereon," enclosure in Dinsmore to Bayard, November 11, 1887, No. 71, United States, Department of State, Despatches from United States Ministers to Korea, 1883–1905 (File Microcopies of Records in the National Archives, Washington, D.C.: No. 134), Roll 4.

42. The chief commissioner of customs, Henry F. Merrill, strongly condemned Yuan's role in Chinese smuggling in Korea. For example, see Merrill to Hart, October 26, 1887, Letterbook 2, Henry F. Merrill Papers, Houghton Library, Harvard University.

43. John H. Mitchell, one of Denny's closest personal friends, was also the single most powerful politician in the state of Oregon between 1872 and 1905. See Robert C. Clark, "John Hipple Mitchell," in *Dictionary of American Biography,* ed. Allen Johnson and Dumas Malone, 20 vols. (New York: Charles Scribner's Sons, 1928–36), 7:53–54.

44. Denny was mistaken in his belief that Dinsmore would have no problem in getting State Department approval. Secretary of State Thomas F. Bayard refused to give Dinsmore permission to accept the Korean position, maintaining that such a change would create special problems for the minister's successor while unnecessarily involving the United States in domestic Korean affairs. Bayard to Dinsmore, March 21, 1888, No. 67, United States, Department of State, Diplomatic Instructions of the Department of State, 1801–1906: Korea (File Microcopies of Records in the National Archives, Washington, D.C.: No. 77), Roll 109.

45. Denny was referring to William H. Parker, who served as U.S. minister to Korea for less than three months (June 12, 1886–September 1, 1886) because of an alcoholic condition. Denny's anger was probably directed toward W. W. Rockhill, who during his stay in Seoul as America's chargé d'affaires did almost nothing to support Korean independence.

46. This description by Denny of "Colonel" Charles Chaillé-Long, then secretary of the U.S. Legation, was not far off the mark.

47. Denny, as a loyal Republican, did not think much of George McClellan, a Civil War general who was the Democratic Party's presidential candidate against Abraham Lincoln in 1864. On the other hand, Ulysses S. Grant, as a Republican Civil War general and later President of the United States, was one of Denny's heroes. They actually became good friends during Grant's visit to China in the late 1870s when Denny was stationed at Tientsin.

48. Denny was referring to his pamphlet, *China and Korea*. See Appendix B.

49. Here Denny was talking about the "spoils system," in which elected American officials could pay off political debts by appointing their friends to diplomatic posts abroad.

50. Denny was not concerned solely with American rights in China. He was also a strong supporter of the rights of Chinese immigrants in the United States. See Robert R. Swartout, Jr., "In Defense of the West's Chinese: Owen N. Denny's Brief to Li Hung-chang," *Oregon Historical Quarterly* 83 (Spring 1982):25–36.

51. Denny was referring to Charles Denby, then U.S. minister to China. See Denny to Mitchell, May 13, 1888, Letter 25.

52. This was the United States presidential race of 1888 between Democrat Grover Cleveland and Republican Benjamin Harrison. Harrison won the election.

53. Secretary of State Bayard denied to Senator Mitchell that he had ever received a despatch from Minister Denby criticizing the American community in Seoul. Yet contrary to this denial, Denby had written the Secretary of State on December 9, 1887: "It is apparent that citizens of the United States have attained great prominence in the agitation of the subject of Corean independence. Is such prominence desirable? Will it be beneficial to us? Will it compensate us for the loss of the good will of China? [Denby's answer to these questions was a firm no.] As the sending of an envoy from Corea to the United States is now assured, this would be a favorable time to bring about the cessation of agitation of ulterior questions, if such policy is desired." See Bayard to Mitchell, June 22, 1888, Letterbook 8, Bayard Papers; Denby to Bayard, December 9, 1887, No. 521, in Palmer, ed., *Korean-American Relations*, p. 110.

54. The U.S. minister to Japan was Richard B. Hubbard, whose own views of Asia may be examined in his *The United States and the Far East: Or, Modern Japan and the Orient* (Richmond, Va.: B. F. Johnson Publishing Co., 1899).

55. Mitchell in fact presented Denny's pamphlet before the U.S. Senate. Both Mitchell's introduction and the pamphlet were printed in the *Congressional Record* (50th Cong., 1st sess., vol. 19, pt. 9, August 31, 1888, pp. 8136–40). Denny's booklet published later in the year by Kelly & Walsh of Shanghai (*China and Korea*) was a revision of this paper and thus contains some material not included in the *Congressional Record*.

As for Mitchell, the senator was using Denny's criticism of China's Korean policy to attack China for domestic reasons. He was one of the West Coast's major backers of the Chinese exclusion acts of the 1880s.

56. For a copy of the June 30, 1888, article in the *Chinese Times* of Tientsin, see Appendix A, Article 1.

57. See also Appendix B for Denny's entire argument on this point.

58. King Kojong had dispatched Min Yŏng-jun as Korea's resident minister to Japan in July 1887.

59. On the issue of sending Korean ministers to Europe and America, see Swartout, *Mandarins, Gunboats, and Power Politics*, pp. 89–95.

60. On von Moellendorff, see also Denny to Wetmore, July 13, 1886, Letter 3, and note 5, above.

61. The 1876 Treaty of Kanghwa. For a copy of this treaty see *KuHanmal choyak hwich'an*, 18:12–16.

62. Here Denny was referring to Cho Pyŏng-sik. See also Yi Hong-jik, *Kuksa taesajŏn*, p. 1492.

63. For a copy of the July 21, 1888 article in the *Chinese Times* of Tientsin, see Appendix A, Article 2.

64. For a continuation of this quotation see ibid. For more comments by Denny along these lines see Appendix B.

65. For example, see Denny to McCracken, January 7, 1888, Letter 7; Denny to Mitchell, February 6, 1888, Letter 23; Denny to Wetmore, March 22, 1888, Letter 24.

66. On Denny's financial problems see note 12, above.

67. Hugo Grotius (1583–1645) was a Dutch jurist and scholar whose studies were of fundamental importance in the development of modern international law.

68. William Blackstone (1723–80) was a noted British jurist who became especially important for his studies on common law. His ideas, in turn, had a very strong influence on the development of American legal traditions.

69. Emeric de Vattel (1714–67) and Henry Wheaton (1795–1848) were both leading authorities in international law. Denny specifically cited Wheaton because he knew that the Chinese themselves were using Wheaton's *Elements of International Law* to support many of their own cases against Western powers. See also Appendix B.

70. These fifty copies of his pamphlet that Denny referred to were, in effect, the first nearly complete draft of his exposé. Two of these copies are contained in Dinsmore to Bayard, August 24, 1888, No. 127, U.S. Diplomatic Despatches, Korea, Roll 5; Japan, Ministry of Foreign Affairs, Archives in the Japanese Ministry of Foreign Affairs, 1868–1945 (microfilmed for the Library of Congress, Washington, D.C., 1949–51), MT 1.2.1.8. When Denny prepared the Kelly & Walsh edition of his booklet, he added a few items not included in the earlier draft.

Denny of course was incorrect in assuming that the publication of his account would drive Yuan from Korea.

71. On the issue of Korean independence—legal and otherwise—see M. Frederick Nelson, *Korea and the Old Orders in Eastern Asia* (Baton Rouge: Louisiana State University Press, 1945; reprint ed., New York: Russell & Russell, 1967), pp. 87, 93, 195–98, 213–20, 291–94; Swartout, *Mandarins, Gunboats, and Power Politics*, pp. 31, 37–44, 106–21; Key-Hiuk Kim, *The Last Phase of the East Asian World Order*, pp. 4–15, 328–51.

72. Denny never wrote a "second chapter" or a follow-up to his original booklet, *China and Korea*.

73. As we have seen, Denny was correct in his belief that the Chinese could never directly drive him from Korea.

74. For a copy of the September 22, 1888 article in the *Chinese Times* of Tientsin, see Appendix A, Article 3.

75. For a copy of the November 24, 1888 article in *Frank Leslie's Illustrated Newspaper*, see Appendix A, Article 4. The sketches of Denny's house contained in the original publication are not included in Appendix A. They are superseded by the actual photographs of the Denny residence printed in this volume.

76. Denny was referring to Sir Lionel Sackville-West, British minister to the United States in 1888. London was forced to recall Sackville-West when some of his private correspondence concerning domestic American politics was printed in American newspapers just before the 1888 election.

77. For a copy of the December 7, 1888 interview with Denny in the *North China Herald* [the "daily *News*"] of Shanghai, see Appendix A, Article 5.

78. Denny was referring to the efforts of von Moellendorff in 1885.

79. Han Kyu-sŏl.

80. John Lindsley was Everett Frazar's business representative in Yokohama, Japan, and, as many of the following letters illustrate, was much involved in Korean economic development.

81. Mr. Payne negotiated on behalf of Everett Frazar's New York-based firm for various economic rights and concessions in Korea. Note most of the following letters, especially Denny to Frazar, March 22, 1890, Letter 42.

82. See Harrington, *God, Mammon, and the Japanese*, pp. 238–41. Min Yŏng-ik, the adopted nephew of Queen Min, was a leading government official in the late nineteenth century. He was one of Korea's first envoys to be sent abroad after the kingdom opened its doors to the West.

83. The two women whom Allen introduced as wives of the Korean diplomats were not actually prostitutes, but rather *kisaeng*, or entertainers analogous to Japanese geisha.

84. "The business of Mr. Payne in New York" was concerned primarily with a large loan Denny and Frazar were attempting to negotiate with the Korean government. Developmental concessions were also included, however, as the remaining letters in this section clearly demonstrate.

85. On the Pierce affair see Denny to General [Kennedy], July 21, 1889, Letter 10; Denny to Lindsley, October 7, 1889, Letter 34.

86. Extraterritoriality, a basic element of the unequal treaties forced upon the East Asian nations in the nineteenth century, allowed Western courts, usually headed by a consul general, to be established in order to try their fellow countrymen accused of committing crimes in the East Asian nations.

87. Hugh Dinsmore's replacement as U.S. minister to Korea turned out to be Augustine Heard. See Denny to Lindsley, June 1, 1890. Letter 46.

88. On Henry F. Merrill see note 28 above.

89. This map has unfortunately disappeared from the Denny records.

90. In the 1880s and into the 1890s the U.S. Congress, under pressure from West Coast states, passed a series of acts to restrict Chinese immigration to the United States. While these developments were not a direct cause of America's neutral policy toward Korea, they did raise many problems for Sino-American relations. See John W. Cassey, "The Mission of Charles Denby and International Rivalries in the Far East, 1885–1898" (Ph.D. dissertation, University of Southern California, 1959), pp. 34–105.

91. For a copy of the December 30, 1889 article in the *Boston Globe*, see Appendix A, Article 6.

92. Charles L. LeGendre, a naturalized American citizen, had for many years served as adviser to the Japanese government. See Sandra Carol Taylor Caruthers, "Charles LeGendre, American Diplomacy, and Expansionism in Meiji Japan, 1868–1893" (Ph.D. dissertation, University of Colorado, 1966).

93. On this scandal, see Denny to Lindsley, October 7, 1889, Letter 34.

94. For LeGendre's appointment see *Ilsŏngnok: Kojong* [Record of daily reflection: Kojong's reign], 44 vols. (Seoul: Sŏul taehakkyo ch'ulp'anbu edition, 1967–72), 27:70. For information on LeGendre's career in Korea see Caruthers, "Charles LeGendre, American Diplomacy, and Expansionism in Meiji Japan, 1868–1893," pp. 351–64; Kwŏn Sŏk-pong, "Yi Sŏn-dŭk ŭi p'a-Il kwa Ch'ŏngch'ŭk kaeip" [On the Chinese

interference in LeGendre's mission to Japan], *Paeksan hakpo* 8 (June 1970):575–624.

95. For an overall analysis of the Payne-Frazar negotiations with Korea see Swartout, *Mandarins, Gunboats, and Power Politics*, pp. 135–42.

96. For studies of Morse Townsend and Company, and the man who headed it, see Harold F. Cook, "Walter D. Townsend: Pioneer American Businessman in Korea," *Transactions of the Korea Branch of the Royal Asiatic Society* 48 (1973):74–103, and *Pioneer American Businessman in Korea: The Life and Times of Walter Davis Townsend* (Seoul: Royal Asiatic Society, Korea Branch, 1981).

97. LeGendre had been deeply involved in the 1874 Japanese expedition to Taiwan, and Denny thus reasoned that the Chinese would look unkindly upon the appointment of their old foe to a key position in the Korean government.

98. That is, Denny to Frazar, June 1, 1890, Letter 45.

99. Augustine Heard, an American from Massachusetts who had been active in the China trade, served as U.S. minister to Korea from May 1890 to July 1893.

Appendix A

1. "Corea," *Chinese Times* (Tientsin), June 30, 1888, pp. 413–15.

2. "Corea," *Chinese Times* (Tientsin), July 21, 1888, pp. 461–63.

3. "Mr. Denny's Pamphlet," *Chinese Times* (Tientsin), September 22, 1888, pp. 605–07.

4. "Glimpses of Corea," *Frank Leslie's Illustrated Newspaper*, November 24, 1888, pp. 239, 241.

5. "Mr. Denny on Corean Affairs," *North China Herald*, December 7, 1888, pp. 636–37.

6. "Korea Kingless," *Boston Globe*, December 30, 1889, pp. 1–2.

Appendix B

1. Published by Kelly & Walsh, Limited, Printers, Shanghai, 1888. For differing interpretations regarding the political and historiographical implications of Owen Denny's booklet, *China and Korea*, see Nelson, *Korea and the Old Orders in Eastern Asia*, pp. 194–95; Swartout, *Mandarins, Gunboats, and Power Politics*, pp. 108–22.

Selected
Bibliography

Primary Sources

Manuscripts

Allen, Horace N., Papers of. New York Public Library, New York City.
Bayard, Thomas F., Papers of. Library of Congress, Washington, D.C.
Denny, Owen Nickerson, Papers of. Private Collection of William C. Ralston, Portland, Oregon.
————, Papers of. Private Collection of Mrs. Stephanie Scott Williams, Tigard, Oregon.
————, Letterbook of. University of Oregon Library, Eugene, Oregon.
Foulk, George C., Papers of. New York Public Library, New York City.
Hart, Robert, Papers of ("Letters to Various Westerners in Chinese Customs Service, 1865–1910"). The Houghton Library of Harvard College Library, Harvard University, Cambridge, Massachusetts.
Japan, Ministry of Foreign Affairs. Archives in the Japanese Ministry of Foreign Affairs, 1868–1945. Microfilmed for the Library of Congress, Washington, D.C., 1949–51.
Merrill, Henry F., Papers of. The Houghton Library of Harvard College Library, Harvard University.
Shufeldt, Robert Wilson, Papers of. Library of Congress, Washington, D.C.
United States, Department of State. Consular Instructions of the Department of State, Shanghai. Record Group 59, National Archives, Washington, D.C.
————. Despatches from United States Consuls in Seoul, 1886–1906. File Microcopies of Records in the National Archives, Washington, D.C.: No. 167.
————. Despatches from United States Consuls in Shanghai, 1847–1906. File Microcopies of Records in the National Archives, Washington, D.C.: No. 112.
————. Despatches from United States Consuls in Tientsin, 1868–1906. File Microcopies of Records in the National Archives, Washington, D.C.: No. 114.

_____. Despatches from United States Ministers to China, 1843–1906. File Microcopies of Records in the National Archives, Washington, D.C.: No. 92.

_____. Despatches from United States Ministers to Japan, 1855–1906. File Microcopies of Records in the National Archives, Washington, D.C.: No. 133.

_____. Despatches from United States Ministers to Korea, 1883–1905. File Microcopies of Records in the National Archives, Washington, D.C.: No. 134.

_____. Diplomatic Instructions of the Department of State, 1801–1906: China. File Microcopies of Records in the National Archives, Washington, D.C.: No. 77.

_____. Diplomatic Instructions of the Department of State, 1801–1906: Japan. File Microcopies of Records in the National Archives, Washington, D.C.: No. 77.

_____. Diplomatic Instructions of the Department of State, 1801–1906: Korea. File Microcopies of Records in the National Archives, Washington, D.C.: No. 77.

_____. Notes from the Korean Legation in the United States to the Department of State, 1883–1906. File Microcopies of Records in the National Archives, Washington, D.C.: No. 166.

_____. Notes to Foreign Legations in the United States from Department of State, 1834–1906: Korea, Persia, and Siam. File Microcopies of Records in the National Archives, Washington, D.C.: No. 99.

Government Publications

Great Britain, Foreign Office. *British and Foreign State Papers, 1886–1887.* Vol. 78. London: William Ridgway, 1894.

_____. Confidential print 5207. *Correspondence Respecting the Temporary Occupation of Port Hamilton by Her Majesty's Government.* Part 1. London: Foreign Office, 1886.

_____. Confidential print 5382. *Further Correspondence Respecting the Temporary Occupation of Port Hamilton by Her Majesty's Government.* Part 2. London: Foreign Office, 1887.

_____. Confidential print 5633. *Further Correspondence Respecting the Temporary Occupation of Port Hamilton by Her Majesty's Government.* Part 3. London: Foreign Office, 1888.

Great Britain, Parliament. Papers by Command. *Correspondence Respecting the Temporary Occupation of Port Hamilton by Her Majesty's Government* [Sessional Papers, 91:87–133]. London: Her Majesty's Stationary Office, 1887.

———. *Hansard's Parliamentary Debates*. Commons, 3rd Series, Vol. 310, 1887.

Japan, Gaimushō [Ministry of Foreign Affairs]. *Dai Nihon gaikō bunsho* [Japanese diplomatic documents]. 73 vols. Tokyo: Nihon kokusai rengyō kyōkai, 1936–63. Vols. 19–21.

Korea, Oemubu chŏngmuguk [Ministry of Foreign Affairs]. *KuHanmal oegyo munsŏ: Miguk kwan'gye p'yŏn* [Diplomatic documents of the late Yi dynasty: American correspondence]. Seoul: Tonga ch'ulp'ansa, 1960.

United States, Congress. *Congressional Record*. 50th Cong., 1st sess., vol. 19, pt. 9, 1888.

———. House. *Investigation of George F. Seward*. H. Rpt. 134, 45th Cong., 3rd sess., 1879.

———. House. *George F. Seward*. H. Rpt. 141, 45th Cong., 3rd sess., 1879.

———. House. *Rent of Consular Premises in China*. H. Exec. Doc. 171, 48th Cong., 1st sess., 1884.

———. House. *Military Instructors for Corea*. H. Exec. Doc. 163, 48th Cong., 2nd sess., 1885.

———. Senate. *Military Instructors for Corea*. S. Rpt. 1443, 48th Cong., 2nd sess., 1885.

United States, Department of State. *Commercial Relations of the United States with Foreign Countries, 1878–1879*. Washington, D.C.: Government Printing Office, 1880.

———. *Commercial Relations of the United States with Foreign Countries, 1880–1881*. Washington, D.C.: Government Printing Office, 1883.

———. *Papers Relating to the Foreign Relations of the United States, 1883*. Washington, D.C.: Government Printing Office, 1884.

———. *Papers Relating to the Foreign Relations of the United States, 1884*. Washington, D.C.: Government Printing Office, 1885.

———. *Papers Relating to the Foreign Relations of the United States, 1888*. 2 vols. Washington, D.C.: Government Printing Office, 1889.

General Document Collections

Carnegie Endowment for International Peace. *Korea: Treaties and Agreements*. Washington, D.C.: The Endowment, 1921.

Chung, Henry, comp. *Korea Treaties*. New York: H. S. Nichols, 1919.

Ilsŏngnok: Kojong [Record of daily reflection: Kojong's reign]. 44 vols. Seoul: Sŏul taehakkyo ch'ulp'anbu edition, 1967–72.

Kojong Sunjong sillok [The veritable record of Kojong and Sunjong]. 3 vols. Seoul: T'amgudang, 1970.

Koryŏ taehakkyo Asea munje yŏn'guso, ed. [Korea University Asiatic Research Center]. *KuHan'guk oegyo munsŏ* [Documents relating to the foreign relations of old Korea]. 22 vols. Seoul: Koryŏ taehakkyo ch'ulp'ansa, 1965–73.

Kransy Archiv. "First Steps in Russian Imperialism in Far East." *Chinese Social and Political Science Review* 18 (July 1934):236–81.

KuHanmal choyak hwich'an [Treaties of the late Yi dynasty]. Seoul: Kukhoe tosŏgwan, 1965.

McCune, George M., and Harrison, John A., eds. *Korean-American Relations: Documents Pertaining to the Far Eastern Diplomacy of the United States, Vol. I: The Initial Period, 1883–1886.* Berkeley and Los Angeles: University of California Press, 1951.

Palmer, Spencer J., ed. *Korean-American Relations: Documents Pertaining to the Far Eastern Diplomacy of the United States, Vol. II: The Period of Growing Influence, 1887–1895.* Berkeley and Los Angeles: University of California Press, 1963.

Sŭngjŏngwŏn ilgi: Kojong [Records of the Royal Secretariat: Kojong's reign]. 15 vols. Seoul: Kuksa p'yŏnch'an wiwŏnhoe edition, 1967–68.

Personal Accounts

Allen, Horace N. *Korea: Fact and Fancy*. Seoul: Methodist Publishing House, 1904.

———. *Things Korean: A Collection of Sketches and Anecdotes, Missionary and Diplomatic*. New York: Fleming H. Revell Company, 1908.

Appenzeller, Henry G., ed. "The Opening of Korea: Admiral Shufeldt's Account of It." *Korean Repository* 1 (February 1892):57–62.

Chaillé-Long, [Charles]. *My Life in Four Continents*. 2 vols. London: Hutchinson and Co., 1912.

Curzon, George N. *Problems of the Far East: Japan—China—Korea*. New York: Longmans, Green and Co., 1896.

Denny, O. N. *China and Korea*. Shanghai: Kelly & Walsh, 1888.

Duncan, Chesney. *Corea and the Powers: A Review of the Far Eastern Question*. Shanghai: "Shanghai Mercury" Office, 1889.

Frazar, Everett. *Korea, and Her Relations to China, Japan and the United States*. Orange, N.J.: Chronicle Book and Job Printing Office, 1884.

Gifford, Daniel L. "John W. Heron, M.D." *Korean Repository* 4 (December 1897):441–43.

Gilmore, George William. *Korea from Its Capital*. Philadelphia: Presbyterian Board of Publication, 1892.

Hart, Robert. *The I. G. in Peking: Letters of Robert Hart, Chinese Maritime Customs, 1868–1907.* Ed. John K. Fairbank, Katherine F. Bruner, Elizabeth M. Matheson. 2 vols. Cambridge: The Belknap Press of Harvard University Press, 1975.

Hubbard, Richard B. *The United States and the Far East: Or, Modern Japan and the Orient.* Richmond, Va.: B. F. Johnson Publishing Co., 1899.

Lowell, Percival. "A Korean Coup d'Etat." *Atlantic Monthly* 58 (November 1886):599–618.

Ramm, Agatha, ed. *The Political Correspondence of Mr. Gladstone and Lord Granville, 1876–1886.* 2 vols. Oxford: The Clarendon Press, 1962.

Sands, William F. *Undiplomatic Memories: The Far East, 1896–1904.* London: John Hamilton, Ltd., n.d.; reprint ed., Seoul: Kyung-In Publishing Co., 1975.

Underwood, Lillias. *Underwood of Korea: Being an Intimate Record of the Life and Work of the Rev. H. G. Underwood.* New York: Fleming H. Revell Co., 1918.

Yun Ch'i-ho. *Yun Ch'i-ho ilgi* [Yun Ch'i-ho's diary]. Ed. Kuksa p'yŏnch'an wiwŏnhoe [National History Compilation Committee]. 6 vols. Seoul: T'amgudang, 1973–76.

Newspapers

Boston Globe.
China Mail (Hong Kong).
Chinese Times (Tientsin).
Frank Leslie's Illustrated Newspaper.
Japan Weekly Mail (Yokohama).
Morning Oregonian (Portland).
New York Daily Tribune.
New York Herald.
New York Times.
North China Herald (Shanghai).
San Francisco Chronicle.
Times (London).

Secondary Sources

Books

Beauchamp, Edward R. *An American Teacher in Early Meiji Japan.* Honolulu: The University Press of Hawaii, 1976.

Bland, J. O. P. *Li Hung-chang*. London: Constable & Company, 1917.

Campbell, Charles S. *The Transformation of American Foreign Relations, 1865–1900*. New York: Harper & Row, 1976.

Ch'en, Jerome. *Yuan Shih-k'ai*. 2nd ed. Stanford: Stanford University Press, 1972.

Chien, Frederick Foo. *The Opening of Korea: A Study of Chinese Diplomacy, 1876–1885*. Hamden, Conn.: The Shoe String Press, 1967.

Choe, Ching Young. *The Rule of the Taewŏn'gun, 1864–1873: Restoration in Yi Korea*. Cambridge: East Asian Research Center, Harvard University, 1972.

Ch'oe Yŏng-hŭi [Choe Young Hee] et al., eds. *Han'guksa* [History of Korea]. 24 vols. Seoul: Kuksa p'yŏnch'an wiwŏnhoe, 1975–78.

Chŏn Hae-jong. *Han-Chung kwan'gyesa yŏn'gu* [A study on the history of Sino-Korean relations]. Seoul: Ilchogak, 1970.

Chŏng Yong-sŏk. *Miguk ŭi taeHan chŏngch'aek, 1845–1980* [The two Korean policies of the United States, 1845–1980]. Seoul: Ilchogak, 1979.

Conroy, Hilary. *The Japanese Seizure of Korea, 1868–1910: A Study of Realism and Idealism in International Relations*. 1st paperback ed. Philadelphia: University of Pennsylvania Press, 1974.

Cook, Harold F. *Korea's 1884 Incident: Its Background and Kim Ok-kyun's Elusive Dream*. Seoul: Royal Asiatic Society, Korea Branch, 1972.

———. *Pioneer American Businessman in Korea: The Life and Times of Walter Davis Townsend*. Seoul: Royal Asiatic Society, Korea Branch, 1981.

Cordier, Henri. *Histoire des Relations de la Chine avec les Puissances Occidentales, 1860–1902*. 3 vols. Paris: Félix Alcan, Éditeur, 1902.

Dallet, Charles. *Histoire de l'église de Corée*. 2 vols. Paris: V. Palme, 1874; reprint ed., Seoul: Kyung-In Publishing Company, 1975.

Dennett, Tyler. *Americans in Eastern Asia: A Critical Study of the Policy of the United States with Reference to China, Japan and Korea in the 19th Century*. New York: The Macmillan Company, 1922.

Deuchler, Martina. *Confucian Gentlemen and Barbarian Envoys: The Opening of Korea, 1875–1885*. Seattle: University of Washington Press, 1977.

Fairbank, John K.; Reischauer, Edwin O.; Craig, Albert M. *East Asia: The Modern Transformation*. Boston: Houghton Mifflin Company, 1965.

Gaston, Joseph. *Portland, Oregon: Its History and Builders*. 3 vols. Chicago: The S. J. Clark Publishing Co., 1911.

Griffis, William E. *Korea: The Hermit Nation*. 8th ed. New York: Charles Scribner's Sons, 1907.

Hahm Pyong-Choon. *The Korean Political Tradition and Law*. 2nd ed. Seoul: Royal Asiatic Society, Korea Branch, 1971.

Han, Woo-keun. *The History of Korea*. Seoul: The Eul-Yoo Publishing Company, 1970.

Harrington, Fred Harvey. *God, Mammon, and the Japanese: Dr. Horace N. Allen and Korean-American Relations, 1884–1905*. Madison: University of Wisconsin Press, 1944.

Henthorn, William. *A History of Korea*. New York: The Free Press, 1971.

Hines, H. K. *An Illustrated History of the State of Oregon*. Chicago: The Lewis Publishing Co., 1893.

Holmgren, Virginia C. *Chinese Pheasants, Oregon Pioneers*. Portland: Oregon Historical Society, 1964.

Hsü, Immanuel C. Y. *China's Entrance into the Family of Nations: The Diplomatic Phase, 1858–1880*. Cambridge: Harvard University Press, 1960.

Hulbert, Homer B. *Hulbert's History of Korea*. Ed. Clarence N. Weems. 2 vols. New York: Hillary House Publishers, 1962.

Kennedy, Thomas L. *The Arms of Kiangnan: Modernization in the Chinese Ordinance Industry, 1860–1895*. Boulder, Colo.: Westview Press, 1978.

Kiernan, E. V. G. *British Diplomacy in China, 1880–1885*. Cambridge: The University Press, 1939.

Kim, C. I. Eugene, and Kim, Han-kyo. *Korea and the Politics of Imperialism, 1876–1910*. Berkeley and Los Angeles: University of California Press, 1967.

Kim Hŭi-il. *Mijenŭn Chosŏn inmin ŭi ch'ŏlch'ŏn ŭi wŏnssu* [The Korean people's grievances against American imperialism]. P'yŏngyang: Choguk t'ong'ilsa, 1969.

Kim, Key-Hiuk. *The Last Phase of the East Asian World Order: Korea, Japan, and the Chinese Empire, 1860–1882*. Berkeley and Los Angeles: University of California Press, 1980.

Kim Wŏn-mo. *Kŭndae Han-Mi kyosŏpsa* [A modern history of Korean-American relations]. Seoul: Hongsŏngsa, 1979.

Lee, Yur-Bok. *Diplomatic Relations Between the United States and Korea, 1866–1887*. New York: Humanities Press, 1970.

Lensen, George A. *Balance of Intrigue: International Rivalry in Korea and Manchuria, 1884–1899*. 2 vols. Gainesville: University Presses of Florida, 1982.

Lin Ming-te. *Yüan Shih-k'ai yü Ch'ao-hsien* [Yuan Shih-k'ai and Korea].

Nan-Kang: Chung yang yen chiu yüan chin tai shih yen chiu so, 1970.

Malozemoff, Andrew. *Russian Far Eastern Policy, 1881–1904: With Special Emphasis on the Causes of the Russo-Japanese War*. Berkeley and Los Angeles: University of California Press, 1958.

Moellendorff, Rosalie von. *P. G. von Moellendorff, Ein Lebensbild*. Leipzig: Otto Harrassowitz, 1930.

Morse, Hosea B. *The International Relations of the Chinese Empire*. 3 vols. London: Longmans, Green, and Co., 1918.

Mun Il-p'yŏng. *Han-Mi osipnyŏnsa* [A fifty-year history of Korean-American relations]. Ed. Yi Kwang-nin. Seoul: Chogwangsa, 1945; reprint ed., Seoul: T'amgudang, 1975.

Nahm, Andrew C., ed. *The United States and Korea: American-Korean Relations, 1866–1976*. Kalamazoo: The Center for Korean Studies, Western Michigan University, 1979.

Nelson, M. Frederick. *Korea and the Old Orders in Eastern Asia*. Baton Rouge: Louisiana State University Press, 1945; reprint ed., New York: Russell & Russell, 1967.

Paik, L. George. *The History of Protestant Missions in Korea, 1832–1910*. 2nd ed. Seoul: Yonsei University Press, 1971.

Pak Il-gŭn. *Kŭndae Han-Mi oegyosa* [A history of modern Korean-American diplomatic relations]. Seoul: Pakusa, 1968.

Palais, James B. *Politics and Policy in Traditional Korea*. Cambridge: Harvard University Press, 1975.

Palmer, Spencer J. *Korea and Christianity: The Problem of Identification with Tradition*. Seoul: Hollym Corporation, Publishers, 1967.

Paullin, Charles O. *Diplomatic Negotiations of American Naval Officers, 1778–1883*. Baltimore: The Johns Hopkins Press, 1912; reprint ed., Gloucester, Mass.: Peter Smith, 1967.

Plesur, Milton. *America's Outward Thrust: Approaches to Foreign Affairs, 1865–1890*. DeKalb: Northern Illinois University Press, 1971.

Rockhill, William W. *China's Intercourse with Korea: From the IXth Century to 1895*. London: Luzac & Co., 1905.

Scott, H. W. *History of Portland, Oregon: With Illustrations and Biographical Sketches of Prominent Citizens and Pioneers*. Syracuse, N.Y.: A. Mason and Co., 1890.

Sin Kuk-chu. *Han'guk kŭndae chŏngch'i oegyosa* [A history of modern Korean politics and diplomacy]. Seoul: T'amgudang, 1968.

Sin Sŏk-ho, ed. *Han'guk hyŏndaesa* [History of modern Korea]. 9 vols. Seoul: Sin'gu munhwasa, 1969.

Spence, Jonathan. *To Change China: Western Advisers in China, 1620–1960*. Boston: Little, Brown & Co., 1969.

Swartout, Robert R., Jr. *Mandarins, Gunboats, and Power Politics: Owen*

Nickerson Denny and the International Rivalries in Korea. Honolulu: The University Press of Hawaii, 1980.

Tansill, Charles. *The Foreign Policy of Thomas F. Bayard, 1885–1897*. New York: Fordham University Press, 1940.

Treat, Payson J. *Diplomatic Relations between the United States and Japan, 1853–1895*. 2 vols. Stanford: Stanford University Press, 1932.

United States, Department of State. *A Historical Summary of United States-Korean Relations*. Washington, D.C.: Government Printing Office, 1962.

Uyehara, Cecil H., comp. *Checklist of Archives in the Japanese Ministry of Foreign Affairs, Tokyo, Japan, 1868–1945*. Washington, D.C.: Library of Congress, 1954.

Varg, Paul A. *Open Door Diplomat: The Life of W. W. Rockhill*. Urbana: The University of Illinois Press, 1952.

Wright, Stanley F. *Hart and the Chinese Customs*. Belfast: Wm. Mullan and Son, 1950.

Yi Hong-jik, ed. *Kuksa taesajŏn* [Encyclopedia of Korean history]. Seoul: Paekmansa, 1975.

Yi Kwang-nin [Lee Kwang-rin]. *Han'guk kaehwasa yŏn'gu* [A study of the history of enlightenment in Korea]. Seoul: Ilchogak, 1969.

Yi Sŏn-gŭn. *Han'guksa ch'oegŭnse p'yŏn* [History of Korea: the modern period]. Seoul: Ŭryu munhwasa, 1961.

Yi Yong-hŭi. *Kŭnse Han'guk oegyo munsŏ ch'ongmok* [Catalogue of foreign diplomatic documents relating to Korea, 1845–1910]. Seoul: Kukhoe tosŏgwan, 1966.

Articles

Bishop, Donald M. "Policy and Personality in Early Korean-American Relations: The Case of George Clayton Foulk." In *The United States and Korea: American-Korean Relations, 1866–1976*, pp. 27–63. Ed. Andrew C. Nahm. Kalamazoo, Michigan: The Center for Korean Studies, Western Michigan University, 1979.

Ch'oe Si-ho. "Han-Mi ch'ogi oegyo kwan'gye koch'al" [A study of early Korean-American diplomatic relations]. *Chŏngch'i hakpo* 5 (1960):123–37.

Ch'oe Sŏk-u. "Han-Pul choyak kwa sin'gyo chayu" [The Korean-French treaty and religious freedom]. *Sahak yŏn'gu* 21 (September 1969):209–29.

Clark, Robert C. "John Hipple Mitchell." In *Dictionary of American Biography*, 7:53–54. Ed. Allen Johnson and Dumas Malone. 20 vols. New York: Charles Scribner's Sons, 1928–36.

Cook, Harold F. "Early American Contacts with Korea." *Transactions of the Korea Branch of the Royal Asiatic Society* 55 (1980):85–107.

————. "Walter D. Townsend: Pioneer American Businessman in Korea." *Transactions of the Korea Branch of the Royal Asiatic Society* 48 (1973):74–103.

Dennett, Tyler. "American Choices in the Far East in 1882." *American Historical Review* 30 (October 1924):84–108.

————. "Early American Policy in Korea, 1883–7." *Political Science Quarterly* 38 (March 1923):82–103.

Dorwart, Jeffery M. "The Independent Minister: John M. B. Sill and the Struggle against Japanese Expansion in Korea, 1894–1897." *Pacific Historical Review* 44 (November 1975):485–505.

Hail, William J. "Li Hung-chang." In *Eminent Chinese of the Ch'ing Period* (1644–1912), 1:464–71. Ed. Arthur H. Hummel. 2 vols. Washington, D.C.: Library of Congress, 1943.

Hamilton, A. H. "Origins of British Interest in Korea in the Nineteenth Century." *Korea Journal* 14 (May 1974):25–33.

Han U-gŭn. "Shufeldt chedok ŭi Han-Mi suho choyak kyosŏp ch'ujin yŏnyu e taehayŏ" [A study on the reasons for sending Commodore Shufeldt to open negotiations with Korea in 1880]. *Chindan hakpo* 24 (August 1963):7–22.

"His Majesty, The King of Korea." *Korean Repository* 3 (November 1896):423–30.

Hong, Soon C. "The Kapsin Coup and Foote: The Role of an American Diplomat." *Koreana Quarterly* 15 (Fall–Winter 1973):60–70.

Hulbert, Homer B. "George Foulk." *Korea Review* 1 (1901):344–49.

Iriye, Akira. "Imperialism in East Asia." In *Modern East Asia: Essays in Interpretation*, pp. 122–50. Ed. James B. Crowley. New York: Harcourt, Brace & World, 1970.

Kennedy, Thomas L. "Self-Strengthening: An Analysis Based on Some Recent Writings." *Ch'ing-shih wen-t'i* 3 (November 1974):3–35.

Ko Pyŏng-ik. "Chosŏn hae'gwan kwa Ch'ŏngguk hae'gwan kwa ŭi kwan'gye—Merrill kwa Hart rŭl chungsim ŭro" [The relationship between the Korean and Chinese Customs Service: Merrill and Hart]. *Tonga munhwa* 4 (October 1965):1–29.

————. "Mok In-dŏk ŭi kobing kwa kŭ paegyŏng" [Von Moellendorff's employment and its background]. *Chindan hakpo* 25–27 (December 1964):225–44.

Kwŏn Sŏk-pong. "Imo gunbyŏn" [The 1882 military riot]. In *Han'guksa* [History of Korea], 16:392–441. Ed. Ch'oe Yŏng-hŭi et al. 24 vols. Seoul: Kuksa p'yŏnch'an wiwŏnhoe, 1975–78.

————. "Yi Sŏn-dŭk ŭi p'a-Il kwa Ch'ŏngch'ŭk kaeip" [On the Chinese interference in LeGendre's mission to Japan]. *Paeksan hakpo* 8 (June 1970):575–624.

Lew, Young I. "American Advisers in Korea, 1885–1894: Anatomy of Failure." In *The United States and Korea: American-Korean Relations, 1866–1976*, pp. 64–90. Ed. Andrew C. Nahm. Kalamazoo, Michigan: The Center for Korean Studies, Western Michigan University, 1979.

———. "The Shufeldt Treaty and Early Korean-American Interaction, 1882–1905." In *After One Hundred Years: Continuity and Change in Korean-American Relations*, pp. 3–27. Ed. Sung-joo Han. Seoul: Asiatic Research Center, Korea University, 1982.

Lin, T. C. "Li Hung-chang: His Korean Policies, 1870–1885." *Chinese Social and Political Science Review* 19 (July 1935):202–33.

Noble, Harold J. "The Korean Mission to the United States in 1883." *Transactions of the Korea Branch of the Royal Asiatic Society* 18 (1929):1–27.

———. "The United States and Sino-Korean Relations, 1885–1887." *Pacific Historical Review* 2 (1933):292–304.

Pollard, Robert T. "America's Relations with Korea, 1882–1895." *Chinese Social and Political Science Review* 16 (October 1932):425–71.

"The Ports and Trade of Corea." *Edinburgh Review* 162 (July 1885):265–85.

Shippee, Lester B. "Thomas Francis Bayard," In *The American Secretaries of State and Their Diplomacy*, 8:47–106. Ed. Samuel Flagg Bemis. 10 vols. New York: Pageant Book Co., 1958.

Sohn Pow-key. "The Opening of Korea: A Conflict of Traditions." *Transactions of the Korea Branch of the Royal Asiatic Society* 36 (1960):101–28.

Song Pyŏng-gi. "Sipgu segimal ŭi yŏnmiron sosŏl: Yi Hong-jang ŭi milhamŭl chungsim ŭro" [An introduction to *The Korean Alliance with America* in the late nineteenth century: centering on Li Hung-chang's confidential letters]. *Sahakchi* 9 (November 1975):61–88.

Swartout, Robert R., Jr. "Cultural Conflict and Gunboat Diplomacy: The Development of the 1871 Korean-American Incident." *Journal of Social Sciences and Humanities* 43 (June 1976):117–69.

———. "In Defense of the West's Chinese: Owen N. Denny's Brief to Li Hung-chang." *Oregon Historical Quarterly* 83 (Spring 1982):25–36.

———. "United States Ministers to Korea, 1882–1905: The Loss of American Innocence." *Transactions of the Royal Asiatic Society, Korea Branch* 57 (1982):29–40

Treat, Payson J. "China and Korea, 1885–1894." *Political Science Quarterly* 49 (December 1934):506–43.

Tsiang, T. F. "Sino-Japanese Diplomatic Relations, 1870–1894." *Chinese Social and Political Science Review* 17 (April 1933):1–106.

Walter, Gary D. "1883nyŏn Mihapjung'guk e p'agyŏn twen TaeChosŏn'guk t'ŭkbyŏl sajŏldan kwanhan yŏn'gu" [A study on the Korean special mission to the United States in 1883]. *Asea hakpo* 6 (June 1969):174–222.

Wright, Mary C. "Adaptability of Ch'ing Diplomacy: The Case of Korea." *Journal of Asian Studies* 17 (May 1958):363–81.

Yi Kwang-nin [Lee Kwang-rin]. "Miguk kunsa kyogwan ŭi ch'obing kwa yŏnmugong'wŏn" [The employment of American military instructors and the military training grounds]. *Chindan hakpo* 23 (1965):7–36.

Yi Po-hyŏng. "Shufeldt chedok kwa 1880nyŏn ŭi Han-Mi kyosŏp" [Commodore Shufeldt and the attempt to open Korea in 1880]. *Yŏksa hakpo* 15 (September 1961):61–91.

Yi Tŏk-kyo. "Sipgu segi huban ŭi Chosŏn bando wa oese ŭi kaldŭng" [Foreign rivalries and the Korean peninsula in the second half of the nineteenth century]. *Chŏngch'i hakpo* 4 (1959):99–111.

Yi Yong-hŭi. "Kŏmundo chŏmryŏng oegyo chonggo" [Diplomacy respecting the occupation of Kŏmundo]. In *Yi Sang-baek Paksa hoegap ki'nyŏmnon ch'ong* [Essay collection in commemoration of the sixtieth birthday of Dr. Yi Sang-baek], pp. 459–99. Seoul: Ŭryu munhwasa, 1964.

Yim, Dong Jae. "The Abduction of the Taewŏn'gun: 1882." *Papers on China* 21 (February 1968):99–130.

Yu Hong-nyŏl. "Kapsin chŏngbyŏn" [The 1884 political coup]. In *Han'guksa* [History of Korea], 16:500–50. Ed. Ch'oe Yŏng-hŭi et al. 24 vols. Seoul: Kuksa p'yŏnch'an wiwŏnhoe, 1975–78.

Dissertations, Theses, and Other Manuscripts

Bishop, Donald M. "Sustaining Korean Independence: American Military Missions to Korea, 1882–1896." M.A. Thesis, Ohio State University, 1974.

Caruthers, Sandra Carol Taylor. "Charles LeGendre, American Diplomacy and Expansionism in Meiji Japan, 1868–1893." Ph.D. dissertation, University of Colorado, 1966.

Cassey, John W. "The Mission of Charles Denby and International Rivalries in the Far East, 1885–1898." Ph.D. dissertation, University of Southern California, 1959.

Hail, William J. Unfinished manuscript biography of Li Hung-chang.

Yale Historical Manuscript Collection, Sterling Memorial Library, Yale University.

Jones, Francis C. "Foreign Diplomacy in Korea, 1866–1894." Ph.D. dissertation, Harvard University, 1935.

Kim, Dalchoong. "Korea's Quest for Reform and Diplomacy in the 1880's: With Special Reference to Chinese Intervention and Controls." Ph.D. dissertation, Fletcher School of Law and Diplomacy, 1972.

Kim, Yung Chung. "Great Britain and Korea, 1883–1887." Ph.D. dissertation, Indiana University, 1965.

Lee, Yur-Bok. "Korean Relations with the United States, 1887–1889: A Study of Conflict Between Old Confucian World Order and Modern International Relations." A paper presented at the 32nd Annual Meeting of the Association for Asian Studies, Washington, D.C., March 21–23, 1980.

————. "Von Möllendorff and Big Power Intervention in Korea in the 1880s." A paper presented at the 29th Annual Meeting of the Midwest Conference on Asian Affairs, University of Iowa, October 24–25, 1980.

Macdonald, Donald Ross H. "Russian Interest in Korea to 1895." Ph.D. dissertation, Harvard University, 1957.

Noble, Harold J. "Korea and Her Relations with the United States before 1895." Ph.D. dissertation, University of California, 1931.

Reordan, Robert E. "The Role of George Clayton Foulk in United States-Korean Relations, 1884–1887." Ph.D. dissertation, Fordham University, 1955.

Woo, Philip M. "The Historical Development of Korean Tariff and Customs Administration, 1875–1958." Ph.D. dissertation, New York University, 1963.

Index

Advisers: American 2–4, 168–69 (n. 14), 170 (n. 28); Korea's decision to employ, 2–3; Western, 163 (n. 9), 167 (n. 5). *See also* Denny, Owen Nickerson

Allen, Horace N.: as Denny's physician, 23; and Korean employment of Pierce, 28; and controversy over Korean legation in Washington, 94; Denny's criticism of, 99, 105, 112

Annam, 141

Austin, John: quoted in *China and Korea*, 141

Barbary States, 142

Bayard, Thomas F., Secretary of State, 46–47, 48, 49–50; policy of neutrality toward Korea, 12, 172 (n. 44), 173 (n. 53)

Bevin, H. M.: Denny's letters to, 31–33

Blackstone, William, 80, 174 (n. 68)

Blaine, James G., Secretary of State, 94, 137

Bluntschli, Johann Kasper: quoted in *China and Korea*, 149

Boston Globe: Denny's criticism of, 107; describes Korean political crisis, 135–38

Brown, R. M., 167 (n. 6); Denny's letter to, 21–22

Bulgaria, 152

Burma, 141, 142

Carpenter, Frank G., 107

Chaillé-Long, Charles, secretary of U.S. legation in Seoul, 25–27, 46–47, 169 (n. 15), 172 (n. 46)

Chefoo, 19, 76, 82

Chemulp'o, 21, 43, 45, 93, 101, 104, 112, 137, 138

China: sends troops to Korea, 3; new Korean policy under Li, 3–4; Self-Strengthening Movement in, 5; opposes dispatch of Korean missions abroad, 9, 72–73, 128, 150–53; and attempts to remove Denny from Korea, 10–11, 81–82; and British occupation of Port Hamilton, 37–40, 43; traditional ties with Korea, 88–89, 123–26, 129–30, 132–33, 142; stifles development of Korea, 101, 158–59. *See also* Li Hung-chang; Yuan Shih-k'ai

China and Korea (essay by Denny), 13, 71–90 passim; publication of, 9, 78–80, 88; Denny's defense of, 79–80, 82–86; *Chinese Times'* critique of, 126–30; reprint of, 139–61; and legalistic interpretation of Sino-Korean relations, 140–53. *See also* Denny, Owen Nickerson

China Merchants Steamship Company, 102

Chinese immigration to United States, 106, 173 (nn. 50, 55), 176 (n. 90)

Chinese pheasants. *See* Pheasants, Chinese

Chinese Times, 72; Denny's criticism of, 77–78, 80; Denny's letter to, 82–86; describes Korean politics, 119–23; on Korean sovereignty, 123–26, 128–30; criticizes Yuan, 125–26; critiques *China and Korea*, 126–30; defends Yuan, 128–30

Cho Pyŏng-sik, 174 (n. 62)

Chou Fu, 168 (n. 11); Denny's letter to, 24–25

Cleveland, Grover, 106, 173 (n. 52)

Cummins, Edmund H., 137, 168–69 (n. 14)

DeLashmutt, Van B., 23, 168 (n. 10); Denny's letter to, 33

Denby, Charles, U.S. Minister to China: criticized by Denny, 49–50; criticizes Americans in Seoul, 173 (n. 53)

Denny, Christian and Eliza (parents), 4

Denny, Gertrude (Mrs. Owen N.), 4, 13, 43, 164 (n. 12)

Sino-Korean commercial agreement (1882), 143, 144–46
Smuggling, Chinese charged with, 45, 129, 154–55, 172 (n. 42)
Spoils system, 173 (n. 49)

Taedong (Tatong) River, 21, 102–03, 112, 158
Taewŏn'gun, 40, 129, 155; exclusionist policy of, 1; political following of, 119–20, 122
Telegraph line in Korea: Denny's support of, 107
Tientsin, 22, 71, 76, 81, 109; Denny appointed U.S. Consul at, 4–5; Denny's visits to, 40–41, 42–43, 75, 87, 156
Tong Shao-yi, secretary of Chinese legation in Seoul, 25, 75
Tumen River, 8, 103

Underwood, Horace G., 23, 168 (n. 8)
United States: and relations with Korea, 1–2, 142–43, 146–48; policy of non-involvement in Korea, 11–12, 172 (n. 44), 173 (n. 53); policy toward China, 48, 176 (n. 90); and Chinese immigration issue, 106, 173 (nn. 50, 55), 176 (n. 90)
United States Department of State: and Denny's dispute with Seward, 5–6; policy toward Korea, 11–12
United States legation, in Seoul: troubles at, 25–27

Vattel, Emeric de, 80, 126, 149, 174 (n. 69)

Vladivostok, 107

Waeber, Karl, Russian chargé d'affaires in Seoul, 104, 170 (n. 25); and Russo-Korean trade agreement, 8, 90, 135
Wetmore, William S., 28, 44, 167 (n. 4); Denny's letters to, 19–21, 47–48, 78–80
Wharton, Francis: quoted in *China and Korea*, 147
Wheaton, Henry, 80, 126, 128, 140, 141, 149, 174 (n. 69); quoted in *China and Korea*, 142
Windsor House (Yokohama): the Dennys and fire at, 167 (n. 1)

Yangban: criticized by Denny, 160, 166 (n. 38)
Yi dynasty, 1
Yi Ha-ŭng. *See* Taewŏn'gun
Yokohama, 47, 93, 103, 167 (n. 1)
Yuan Shih-k'ai: selected to carry out Li's policies, 3; and Denny, discord between, 9, 10–11, 127 (*see also* Yuan Shih-k'ai, Denny's criticism of); attempts to dethrone Kojong, 39–40, 43–44, 129–30, 154, 155–56, 170–71 (n. 30); Denny's criticism of, 39–41, 43–44, 45, 72–75, 81–82, 82–83, 88–90, 100, 128–29, 132–35, 153–58; and smuggling in Korea, 45, 129, 154–55, 172 (n. 42); criticized in *Chinese Times*, 125–26; defended in *Chinese Times*, 128–30. *See also* China; Li Hung-chang

ABOUT THE AUTHOR

Robert R. Swartout, Jr. is associate professor of history and coordi-
nator of the International Relations Program at Carroll College in
Helena, Montana. He received both his bachelor's and master's
degrees from Portland State University and his doctorate from
Washington State University. He is the author of *Mandarins,
Gunboats, and Power Politics: Owen Nickerson Denny and the
International Rivalries in Korea* (1980) and the editor of *Montana
Vistas: Selected Historical Essays* (1981).